The *Horse Illustrated* Guide to

WESTERN RIDING

By Lesley Ward

BOWTIE
PRESS

A Division of BowTie, Inc.
Irvine, California

Karla Austin, Business Operations Manager

Ruth Strother, Editor-At-Large

Erin Kuechenmeister, Production Editor

Rebekah Bryant, Editorial Assistant

Nick Clemente, Special Consultant

Jen Dorsey, Associate Editor

Michelle Martinez, Assistant Editor

Michael Vincent Capozzi, Book Design

The horses in this book are referred to as *he* or *she* in alternating chapters unless their gender is apparent from the activity discussed.

The photograph on page 130 is courtesy of © Bob Langrish.

Text copyright © 1998, 2003 by Lesley Ward. Previously published in a larger format in *The* Horse Illustrated *Guide to Western Riding*.

Library of Congress Cataloging-in-Publication Data

Ward, Lesley.
  The Horse Illustrated guide to western riding / by Lesley Ward.
    p. cm.
  ISBN 1-931993-17-3 (hardcover : alk. paper)
  1. Western riding. I. Title: Guide to western riding. II. Horse
Illustrated. III. Title.

SF309.3.W37 2004
798.2'3--dc21

2003014047

BowTie Press®
A Division of BowTie, Inc.
3 Burroughs
Irvine, California 92618
Printed and bound in Singapore
10 9 8 7 6 5 4 3 2 1

Acknowledgments

I would like to thank the following people for their help with this book: Sarah Deluca; Pat Fuchs; Jennifer Griffin; Diane Harkey; Becky Holman, Black Diamond Performance Horses; Carol Nelson; Jennifer Oltmann; Sherry Pascual; Dale Rudin; Heather Hayes Schram; Firestorm Arabians; Julie Salinas; Erica Seiver; and finally my dad, Alan Ward, for his editing skills.

Contents

Introduction

So you want to learn how to ride western? Once you slip into the comfortable seat of a western saddle, there are many activities to choose from. If you're competitive, you can try your hand at gymkhana games, reining, barrel racing, roping, or team penning. If you're laid-back, you could spend hours exploring the countryside on horseback. If you're sociable, you could enjoy long trail rides and picnics with other horse lovers. Western riding offers something for everyone.

You don't need to be born on a ranch or live in the heart of Texas to become a good western rider, but you do need to be dedicated to improving your horsemanship. Good horsemanship is based on constant communication between horse and rider and the desire to continually improve your riding skills.

When you first learn to ride, you'll be taught how to sit in the saddle, how to hold the reins, and how to make a horse go forward. As you become more secure in the saddle, you'll worry less about falling off and begin to concentrate more on the horse's performance. You'll learn how to give the cues that guide the horse, and as you improve, you'll find that most horses actually listen to you. It takes time and practice in the saddle before you become an effective rider.

If you're just starting out, it's important to sign up with a good riding instructor who will teach you the basics. No matter how experienced you become, you'll never stop learning. Every time you jog down a country road, or land on the ground after a fall, you add to your library of equestrian knowledge.

Use this book in addition to your hands-on experiences. Read it before you head for your lessons and refer back to it as needed. It won't be long before you are riding with confidence. Let's face it—it's easy to get hooked on western riding!

Starting Out

So, going on the occasional trail ride on a rented horse isn't enough for you anymore? If you're serious about learning how to ride and improve your western riding skills, look for a good trainer and sign up for lessons. If you don't have a horse of your own, find a trainer with his own string of horses or one who is based at a riding school. If you do have your own horse but are new to riding, it may be a good idea to board your horse at a barn with an experienced instructor on-site.

Choosing a Riding School

Visit your local tack shop and check the bulletin board. There should be a few signs or business cards advertising local riding schools or trainers. If one catches your eye, write down the phone number. Ask the sales assistant if she can recommend any reputable schools or trainers.

Check the bulletin board to see if western shows are advertised. If there are shows in your area, go hang around the warm-up arena and watch the riders and their trainers in action. If you like the way a particular trainer works with a student, approach him when he is less busy and introduce yourself. Find out if he gives lessons and if he is based at a nearby barn. Most trainers are happy to chat with you. If you like what you hear, arrange to meet at the trainer's barn to take a look at his lesson horses and see how he runs his business.

You can also look in the yellow pages for western riding schools or facilities near you, but don't sign up for lessons until you've seen the place. When you go, stop by the office and let the manager know you've arrived. Ask her if you can look around while lessons are going on. She may offer to give you a tour of the facility or she may send you off by yourself to have a look at the place. As you're walking around, keep the following points in mind:

The Staff: The employees should be friendly and happy to answer your questions. They should be dressed professionally—in jeans and boots, not shorts and sandals. No one should be smoking in the barn area. Workers should be kind but firm with the horses. You shouldn't see people shouting at horses or beating them into submission.

The Barn: The barn should be neat and well organized. You shouldn't spot any litter or loose baling twine lying on the ground.

The barn area should be tidy and safe.

Lesson horses should look clean and well fed.

Manure and used bedding should be swept neatly onto a muck heap, away from the barn. As you walk around, look in some stables and check the cleanliness of the bedding. If horses are standing in piles of manure or puddles of urine, leave and look for a better barn.

The Lesson Horses: The lesson horses should look healthy and alert. They should be fairly well groomed, and their hooves should look like they get regular trimming and shoeing. The horses don't need to look show-quality clean—especially if they live out in a pasture or pen most of the time—but they should look cared for and well fed. You shouldn't be able to see ribs or hip bones sticking out.

Don't sign up for lessons at a barn where the horses look tired and in poor condition. Ask the trainer how many times a day they are ridden. A horse shouldn't be used for more than three lessons a day. You don't want to have a lesson on a worn-out horse that has already been ridden five times in a row.

13

The Lessons: Watch a few lessons. Right away you should notice if the barn matches riders and horses by size and ability. Tiny riders should not be stuck on huge horses, and large riders should not be mounted on ponies. If a rider is petite, he or she may not be able to handle a large, strong horse, and the person's legs may be too short to give effective cues. If a rider is too big or overweight for a small horse, the stable is obviously not interested in the welfare of its lesson horses.

Can everyone in the lesson control the horse he or she is riding? When you're just learning to ride, you don't want to be assigned a frisky, bad-natured horse who will ruin your confidence, or injure you or other members of the class. Lesson horses should be quiet and fairly obedient and should take direction well. But don't be too critical of the horses, either. Because of the variety of novice riders, lesson horses are rarely perfect. They can be sluggish and will sometimes ignore their rider's cues. This is normal. Who can blame them? Being jerked in the mouth by students all day can make even the best-behaved horse slightly grumpy. But if riders seem to be having serious problems with their horses this might not be a reputable barn. You shouldn't see any bucking, kicking, rearing, or bolting in a class for novice riders. If you see frequent examples of this behavior, you might want to shop around for a new school.

Lesson horses should wear simple, well-fitting tack. The equipment doesn't have to be new, but it should be clean and in good condition. Badly worn tack may break and cause an accident, harming both you and the horse. The horses should wear simple snaffle bits or mild curb bits. Severe bits such as a high-port curb, or a tiny twisted wire snaffle are not needed on quiet lesson horses.

And finally, are all the students in the class of the same riding level and approximate age group? If you're a new rider, you don't want to be put in a class with advanced people who are practicing complicated reining patterns. It can be extremely frustrating to be placed in a class with a twelve-year-old barrel-racing champion if

Trainers often advertise on a riding facility's bulletin board.

you are a twenty-five-year old beginner. A good trainer puts students of similar ability together because he'll be able to teach the group more effectively by focusing on skills and tasks that most benefit the education of the entire group.

Choosing a Trainer

If you decide not to go to a riding school but to use an independent trainer instead, don't sign up with the first trainer you meet. Anyone can put up a sign at a barn and declare himself a trainer. There are no licensing boards or testing requirements for

15

Watch your potential trainer as she teaches a class or two.

Students should look as if they're enjoying themselves.

trainers in the United States, and many people are simply not qualified to teach. Do some investigating. If you have friends who ride, ask about their trainers, and watch different trainers teach lessons before you choose one. Often you'll find the best trainers by word of mouth.

When you do find an instructor you are interested in, ask how long he has been teaching and about his riding experiences. He shouldn't mind. A truly qualified trainer will have ridden and competed successfully for many years and will be happy to share his experience with you. Here are qualities you should look for when watching a trainer teach a lesson:

It's best to ride in well-fitting jeans and boots with heels.

- dressed professionally, in jeans and boots
- not afraid to get on a horse to demonstrate what he is talking about
- has a lesson plan and doesn't just sit on the rail, making few remarks
- classes are small (no more than five students) and each rider gets plenty of attention
- students look confident and seem to be enjoying themselves
- classes are varied and students are not doing the same thing over and over
- patient and does not shout at or bully students

To get an idea about the going rate for lessons in your area, ask your friends how much they pay, then if you like a trainer, find out how much he charges. Some trainers will give you a discount if you pay for a series of lessons up front. Ten lessons is usually the norm. Private lessons cost more than group ones, but some trainers want you to sign up for a few private lessons at first so they can concentrate on the basics with you and find out what you can do.

You may have a lesson or two on the lunge line to work on your position without your having to control the horse. After a few private lessons, your trainer should be able to place you in a compatible group. Group lessons can be a lot of fun and a great opportunity to meet like-minded horse people. Sign up for as many lessons as you can afford. If you're really serious about riding, you should take at least one lesson a week.

If you are fortunate enough to have a horse and keep him at home, you have a couple of options. Some trainers may be happy to come to your house and teach you. These lessons may be more expensive because the trainer adds his traveling expenses to your bill. If you plan to take lessons at home, you must have a cleared-off, level area where it is safe to ride. There's no way a trainer can teach you effectively in a hilly pasture or a field covered in knee-high grass. There shouldn't be any rocks on the ground in your riding area either. If you have a trailer, and your trainer is local, you could haul your horse to his barn for lessons. This will be quite time-consuming for you, but your horse benefits by being worked in an arena and getting used to being trailered and being away from home.

What You Should Wear to Ride

When you start lessons, there's no need to buy expensive boots and chaps right away. A pair of well-fitting jeans and boots or low-heeled shoes with laces will do just fine. Sneakers are unacceptable because they have no heels. You need heels to keep your feet from sliding through the stirrups. If one of your feet were to slide through the stirrup and you fell off, your leg might get caught in the stirrup and the horse could drag you.

As you become a more experienced western rider, you may want to add to your wardrobe, especially if you plan to compete in shows. First, you'll need a sturdy pair of riding boots. While the pointed cowboy boot that you see in western stores is fine for fashion, most riders wear roper-style boots. They are pull-on style and feature a rounded toe. There are also lace-up ropers, which are styled similar to a hiking boot, ankle-high and lacing up the front.

You'll also want a hat to protect your head from the sun in summer and to keep it warm in winter. Most western riders wear fur felt or straw hats. Go to a tack shop and try on a few hats to see which style suits you. You will find in the fur felt hats several Xs. These signify how much actual fur is used in creating the hat. The more Xs, the higher quality the hat is. Natural colors are in, with colors like fawn, bone, silverbelly, and bone being as popular as black.

Western riders who are concerned with safety, as we all should be, wear schooling helmets with a fixed harness. Wearing a protective helmet is especially smart if you're a new rider. You never know when you might take a fall. Everyone does—sooner or later.

If you'd like to wear a helmet, but prefer the western style, there is a cowboy hat with a protective shell inside that meets current safety standards and is available in felt or straw. The American Quarter Horse Association (AQHA) has been a leader in encouraging western riders to wear safety helmets, and riders at AQHA shows are allowed to wear them while competing in any class.

If you want to enter a show, you will need a pair of chaps. Chaps (pronounced shaps) are traditionally designed to protect a rider's legs from brush and other trail hazards. They also have the added benefit of keeping the leg warmer in cold weather. But for show they are simply part of the uniform. Most western riders sport fringed chaps. Suede is popular, but synthetic ultrasuede

Offer to groom your lesson horse to gain experience.

chaps are what are found in the show pen. They are designed to sit high on the waist with your belt, and have an elongated heel, called a heel drop, which covers heel and spur when you're in the saddle.

Western fashions are continually evolving, so before investing in shirts or jackets, look at catalogs and at what others are wearing and then develop your own style. For showing, men will need a plain-cut, long-sleeved shirt that buttons down the front and has a collar. Women riders in competitions often wear beautifully tailored, colorful tops and matching pants.

Gaining Experience in the Saddle

Once you've started regular lessons, you may want to spend more time around horses. You'll gain valuable experience and have fun at the same time. Consider a few of the following ways to accomplish this:

Volunteer to exercise horses to get more riding time.

Be early: Arrive early for your lesson and offer to groom and tack up your horse. You may have to watch a groom tack up a few times before you attempt it yourself, but you'll soon get the hang of it. Working one-on-one with your lesson horse is a good way to get to know him. After your lesson, ask if you can untack your horse and feed or water him. Your trainer will appreciate your help.

Exercise other people's horses: Some people are simply too busy to give their horses the exercise they need. Ask your trainer if he knows of anyone who needs some help. If your trainer thinks you are a competent rider, he'll recommend you to people who need their horses exercised.

Be a working student: Some trainers take on working students (people who ride and exercise the trainer's horses in exchange for lessons). If you have a job, you won't have enough time to be a full-time working student, but your trainer may utilize your riding talents in the evenings and on weekends.

Offer to be a horse-sitter: Put up a sign at your facility advertising your services as a horse-sitter. When folks go away on vacation, they might ask you to groom, feed, and turn out their horses. You may get to ride, too, but don't count on it. Ask other people at your facility how much they think you should charge.

Volunteer for the North American Riding for the Handicapped Association (NARHA): There are many riding and driving programs for people with disabilities. These programs always need volunteers. You may be asked to groom and tack up horses. You may lead horses and riders around the ring, or you could be a "sidewalker"—a person who walks next to the lesson horse and helps the rider keep his or her balance and self-confidence. Volunteering for NARHA is a worthwhile use of your time; you'll meet a lot of horse people with big hearts. Contact NARHA to see if there is a program in your area.

Join a trail-riding organization: This is a group of people who get together several times a month and hit the local trails. These rides can have as few as ten participants or more than one hundred, depending on where you live. Trail-riding enthusiasts often take part in "workdays" in which they maintain and repair local trails. They also organize picnics and social activities. Attend some events and get to know people. You may meet someone who is willing to lend you a horse so you can join the fun.

Be a horse-show volunteer: Most shows need volunteers to do things such as open gates, help judges, and move obstacles around in trail and barrel racing classes. Being a volunteer is a super way to learn about shows and study western riders in action. This information will help you when you compete in shows. Look on

Going on a riding vacation can improve your skills in the saddle.

the tack shop bulletin boards to see if there are any shows in your area. Call up the show managers and offer your services. They will probably be thrilled to hear from you.

Be a 4-H volunteer or leader: This youth group often needs adults to help at meetings and shows. Call your county's agricultural extension office to learn who is in charge of the equestrian branch of the local 4-H.

Attend clinics: Many facilities offer clinics given by top riders and trainers. Even if you don't have a horse, you can usually pay a small fee and attend as a spectator. You'll learn a lot about riding and horsemanship simply by watching and listening, and you may be able to ask questions too.

Escape on a riding vacation: Browse through horse magazines to find travel companies that specialize in riding holidays and send for some brochures. You could trail ride through a wildlife park in Kenya, work cattle on a dude ranch in Wyoming, or ride a mule in the Grand Canyon. There are a lot of riding vacations in Great Britain, Ireland, France, Australia, and New Zealand as well.

In the Saddle

When you begin to ride, you may think lessons are a bit dull. Why should you stay in the ring and work on your position while others are out riding the trails and having a great time? Because it's important to learn the basics at the very beginning of your riding career. It may be fun to lope off into the sunset right off the bat, but you won't learn the skills that you need to become a good rider. It is essential that you learn these skills early on in your riding career because it doesn't take long to form bad riding habits that, unfortunately, last you a lifetime. Bad habits, such as slouching in the saddle, yanking on the reins, and constantly poking your horse with your heels, are easy to pick up.

Start out right with an experienced trainer who can show you how to sit properly the first time you mount a horse, who can teach you how to communicate quietly and effectively with your horse, and who can help you become a well-balanced, relaxed rider.

Fit for Riding

You must be fit and flexible if you're going to ride seriously. A rider is an active partner of a horse, not a passive load. You don't have to be as thin as a rake, but you should be in reasonably good shape. Don't expect your horse to gallop down trails and scramble up hills if you'd be hard-pressed to run 50 yards without fainting. You won't be doing your horse any favors if you huff and puff after five minutes of loping. Plus, most western saddles are fairly heavy, and once you've plopped into the seat, your poor horse has even more weight to carry.

Walk next to your horse's shoulder when leading her.

If the reins are looped around the horn, grab hold of them under the horse's neck.

Stay in shape by riding a bike or joining an aerobics class. Round up other riders from your facility and go on a long, healthful walk every day. You can burn up calories and strengthen your muscles around the barn too. Mucking out your horse's stall or lugging bales of hay around is great exercise.

Leading a Horse

Before you mount a horse you need to lead her to the ring or the mounting area. She should be fully tacked up and ready for your lesson. Stand on her left side, facing forward, and hold both reins with your right hand, about 3 inches below her chin. Tradition dictates that you stand on the horse's left, but your horse should get used to being led from both sides because you may need this skill on the trail. Hold the excess rein with your left hand. Don't let them drag on the ground as you walk because your horse could step on them and break them.

Facing the same direction as your horse, stand next to her shoulder. When you begin to walk, she should too. Some horses understand voice commands, so you may want to say "walk" or make a clucking sound. When you want your horse to halt, give a small tug on the reins with your right hand, say "whoa," and stop. If your horse continues walking, give one or two more tugs. If she still won't halt, bend your right arm, stick your elbow in front of her chest to form a barrier, and lean into her. Jab her several times and say "whoa" again.

If your horse is inexperienced, practice leading and halting every time you prepare to ride. A horse that barges in front of you or ignores your command to halt can become dangerous, so enforce the rules the first time you handle her and continue to treat her firmly.

Mounting a Horse

Grabbing the saddle's horn and hauling yourself into the seat inch-by-inch may be the easiest way to mount, but it's not the best way. When you put your full weight on the horn and pull yourself up, you can pull the saddle over sideways and twist the tree, damaging it. You can also put unnecessary strain on your horse and cause her back problems. It's no surprise that many horses fidget when they're mounted badly. Here are some ways to mount that will not damage your expensive saddle or upset your horse.

From the Ground

1. Before you mount, check that the cinch is tight. When you first fasten the cinch, a smart horse sucks air into her stomach, dis-

tending her belly. Then she blows the air out so the cinch is loose. When you try to mount, the saddle slips to one side and you end up on the ground. So always check the cinch first.

2.   Tradition states that riders mount from the left side, but get in the habit of mounting from both sides. You may need to mount from the right on a trail, and you don't want your horse to freak out because you've never done it before. This is important if you ever have to mount on a hill. Always mount on the uphill side, no matter which side of the horse this is.

If the reins are looped around the horn, unloop them and rest them near the withers. Most western reins are split, and it's easy to place both reins together and lay them on the left side of your horse's neck. The same goes for romal reins. Romal reins use a woven leather strip that joins the two reins at their ends and makes them one. It allows the length of the reins to be easily adjusted and is sometimes used as a whip.

Gather the reins in your left hand, then lay your hand on the horse's neck. You can grab hold of some of the mane, too. The reins should be loose enough so you won't bang your horse in the mouth when you mount, but short enough so that you can check her immediately if she starts to move off.

3.   Stand next to the shoulder of the horse and face the rear. This keeps you away from the hind legs. Most horses won't try to kick you as you mount; however, if your horse should move as you swing up, you'll be pulled into the saddle rather than dumped on the ground.

4.   Now use your right hand to turn the stirrup and place the toe of your left foot in the stirrup. If your horse should jump as you're mounting, your toe would come out of the stirrup much easier than your whole foot. As soon as your toe is in the stirrup, put your right hand on the horn—not the cantle—and place your left knee as close to the horse's shoulder as possible.

Face your horse's hindquarters when preparing to mount.

Pivot on your right foot until you're facing your horse's side.

Bounce several times and lift your right leg over your horse's hindquarters.

Sit down gently in the saddle.

5. With your left hand on the neck, your left toe in the stirrup, your left knee against the shoulder, and your right hand on the horn, you're ready to mount. Bounce upward on your right foot—rising quickly—and swing smoothly by pivoting on your left knee. Keep your head and shoulders low. Basically, you're rolling onto the horse. Don't swing your right leg over until your head and shoulders are over the horse.

Another mounting method that can be used on gentle horses is to stand alongside the saddle facing slightly toward the horse's head. Your left hand holds the reins and lies against the neck. Now, using your right hand, put the toe of your left foot in the stirrup, and take hold of the horn. Step up, keeping your right hip against the horse, and throw your right leg over the saddle. Try not to kick your horse in the rump.

6. Settle down in the seat slowly and gently. Humans cause a lot of equine back problems by thumping down into the saddle when mounting, so be gentle and keep your horse's comfort and safety in mind. Slip your right foot into the right stirrup immediately without looking down.

From a Mounting Block

Occasionally you may need help mounting a horse. She might be a very tall horse, or she could have a sensitive back and must be mounted gently, or you could have an injury and need to mount carefully. This is when a mounting block comes in handy. Most barns or riding schools have one handy. Position the horse so her left side is next to the block, ask her to halt, and put your left foot in the stirrup. Then, swing your right leg over her back and gently lower yourself into the saddle. Finally, slip your right foot in the stirrup. Practice mounting from a fence or a log, too so the horse gets used to the process of mounting from an object. Mounting from different objects should not worry your horse.

A mounting block makes it easy to get into the saddle.

Perfecting Your Position

Once you've mounted your horse, you must work on your position—the way in which you sit in the saddle. It's important to establish a correct riding position in your first few lessons because it's the key to becoming an effective rider, not a passenger.

One of your most essential riding goals is to have a "secure seat," which means you stick close to the saddle and don't bounce around and hinder your horse when she's moving. You want to move with your horse, not interfere with her natural way of going.

The way you sit influences the ways she moves. If you lean one way, she'll lean that way too in an effort to carry your weight comfortably. If you fall forward on her neck, you may unbalance her front end and cause her to trip. Try to sit quietly in the saddle and stay in sync with your horse's movements and relax. If you're stiff as a board, you can't be an effective rider.

If you're truly serious about improving your skills, head out to the local shows and watch a lot of different competitors. The successful ones always look like they are doing very little. Their movements are subtle; they look relaxed and comfortable in the saddle. When you ride, think about what these good riders look like and try to emulate their position. It may take a while and you may bounce around occasionally—but don't worry. If you're well taught and you spend enough time in the saddle, maintaining a good position will become second nature to you.

Here's an example of a solid position, starting at the top of the body and working our way down:

Head

Hold your head high and look forward, between your horse's ears. Always look in the direction you're going and keep your eye focused on the road or trail ahead. Looking down or tipping your

Establishing a secure seat should be your number one goal in the first few lessons.

head to one side affects your balance and can influence the way your horse moves. Carry yourself with confidence and keep your chin up.

Shoulders

Don't slouch or hunch over or let one shoulder drop lower than the other. Roll your shoulders back and keep them level.

Chest

Keep your upper body straight. Stick out your chest slightly. Suck in your stomach and try to keep it flat.

Keep your back straight and your head up when working on your position.

Back

Your back should be straight, but not stiff. Keep it flexible and move with your horse.

Arms and Hands

As you begin riding, it's likely you'll be taught to "neck rein," using only your left hand to steer your horse. Most western events require you to use only one hand on the reins, but there are a few exceptions, for example classes in which horses are ridden in snaffles or bosals (a type of hackamore) allow two hands on the reins. You may also need two hands to steer a green (inexperienced or untrained) horse.

Riding with two hands on the reins: When you use two hands on the reins, your upper arms and elbows should be close to your sides. Your lower arms should be parallel, about 5 inches apart. Your hands should be on either side of the horn and slightly in front of it. Grip the reins with the middle three fingers of each hand. Rest your thumbs on top and your pinky fingers under the reins. Face your palms toward each other and turn your knuckles out. Cross the excess reins over the withers.

When your hands and arms are in the correct position, you should be able to imagine a straight line all the way from your forearms through the reins to the bit.

Riding with one hand using split reins: When using only one hand on the reins, your upper arms should also be close to your body.

It's traditional to hold the reins with your left hand because most people are right-handed and use that hand for opening gates or roping livestock. You will not be penalized in show classes for using your right hand, so if you are a lefty do as you please.

There are two ways to hold split reins. The first is with your fist, as if you were holding an ice cream cone. Bring both reins together and hold them in your palm. Wrap four fingers around the reins and rest

You may use two hands on the reins while learning to ride.

your thumb on top. Don't clench your fingers tightly; this causes your arm to stiffen. The second way to hold split reins is to put your pointer finger between the reins. This allows you to manipulate and control the reins more, which comes in handy with horses that don't neck rein well.

Once you have a secure grip on the reins, hold your hand slightly above and in front of the horn. You can hold your hand at a slight angle, but your knuckles should face to the sides for proper form and function. The ends of the reins should fall gently on the left side of the horse. And what about your right hand? Just rest it on your thigh.

When using romal reins, your rein hand should rest slightly above or in front of the horn.

Riding with one hand using romal reins: Hold the two reins together in your left palm and squeeze your four fingers around them. Your thumb goes underneath the reins and rests on top of your other fingers. Hold the single rein end of the romal with your right hand and rest it on your thigh as shown. Once again, your rein hand should rest slightly above or in front of the horn.

Seat

Sit squarely in the middle of the saddle seat. Distribute your body weight evenly over both seat bones. Some trainers call it "riding on your pockets," which gives you a deep, secure feeling in the saddle.

Legs

The first step in getting your legs in the correct position is to adjust your stirrups so they're the right length for you. Many trainers believe that the bottom of the stirrup should be level to, or just below, your anklebone. This can't always be the case, however. If you're riding a fat horse, her size affects your stirrup length; if you are competing in a cutting class or working cattle, you might want a shorter stirrup because it gives you extra security in the saddle.

An easy way to check if your stirrups are the right length is to imagine a straight line running from your ear, down your shoulder, through your upper arm and hip, and down to the back of your heel while you're sitting on the horse. If your stirrups are too long or too short, this line will not be perfectly straight. Ask a friend or your trainer if he can "see" that line along your body. If he can't, you'll have to dismount to adjust the stirrups. Another way to check your stirrup length quickly is to stand up in the stirrups. If they are the right length, you should be able to easily slide your whole hand (palm down) between your rear end and the saddle seat.

Your thighs should rest on the saddle. Your knees should be slightly bent and flat against the saddle, but don't squeeze with

When neck reining, rest your thumb on top of the right rein.

To dismount, take your right foot out of the stirrup and swing your leg over your horse's hindquarters.

Dismount slowly and quietly.

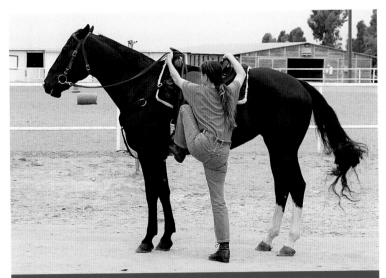

Place your right foot on the ground and take your left foot out of the stirrup.

Loop the ends of the reins around the horn so they don't drop on the ground and get stepped on.

them. Squeezing makes your body stiff and tense and can make you lean too far forward when the horse is moving. Your calves should have a light contact with your horse's sides. Your calves need to be close to her because they give your horse cues and must be able to apply pressure quickly and effectively.

Feet

The balls of your feet should rest on the tread of the stirrup, and your toes should be slightly higher than your heels. Your toes should be pointed forward, not outward. Your feet should be even on each side of your horse.

Dismounting

For most riders, it's a lot easier getting off a horse than on. If you follow these steps, it will be easy for you, too:

1. If you're using a romal, bring it over to the left side of your horse and let it rest next to her neck. Then place both reins in your left hand and shorten them so you have contact on the horse's mouth. Rest your left hand on your horse's neck, near her withers.

2. Place your right hand on the horn and stand up slightly in the saddle. Take your right foot out of the stirrup and slowly swing your right leg over your horse's hindquarters. Keep your shoulders level and look straight ahead.

3. Step down to the ground with your right foot. As your right foot touches the ground, remove your left foot from the stirrup and place it on the ground too. You should be facing the saddle. Take hold of the reins again.

Keeping your calves close to the horse's sides allows you to give her subtle cues.

3

Moving On

As you learn to ride, it's best to start at the walk—the slowest and easiest gait to control. Once you can manage your horse at this sedate pace, you can move on to more energetic activities.

The Aids

During your first lesson, your trainer will explain the cues that let you communicate with and control your horse. These are called aids. There are natural aids and artificial aids. The aids a horse responds to are generally the ones he was taught by his first rider or trainer. This is why a horse may not understand your particular aids, and it's also why it sometimes takes a while for a horse and rider to get used to each other. It takes time and repetition before a horse fully understands your cues.

Natural Aids

Natural aids come from your legs, hands, seat, and voice:

Legs: Squeezing your horse with your lower legs tells him to move forward, sideways, or backward.

Hands: Your hands hold the reins, which attach to the bit. You use your hands to steer a horse or slow him down.

Seat: The way you sit in the saddle affects your horse's movement. When you sit deep and lean back slightly, he may slow down.

Leaning forward over his neck tells him to go faster. Shifting your weight to one side or the other may tell him to turn.

Voice: Some horses are trained to obey voice commands. For example, if you make clucking noises to some horses, they may speed up.

If you say "whoa" or "ho" in a firm voice, they may slow down. Raising your voice slightly and speaking in a sharp tone can inform your horse that he's being naughty.

Artificial Aids

Artificial aids—such as spurs, whips/bats, and the ends of your reins—help your natural aids:

Spurs: Used to give subtle cues to a horse, spurs reinforce leg aids. It takes skill to use spurs correctly. Beginners often use them before they're ready because they're part of the western "look." But if you can't control your legs, you can't control spurs and you'll just poke your horse and make him angry. Work with your trainer to strengthen your leg position before strapping on spurs.

When you begin to use spurs, use short, blunt ones. You don't need sharp spurs with 3-inch shanks. In fact, a short pair of English-style "Tom Thumb" spurs are the best. When riding, use your leg aids first and if your horse ignores them, or doesn't react quickly, increase your leg pressure until the spur touches him. The second your horse responds, remove the spur from his side.

Try not to kick your horse in anger with spurs. Many horses have ugly scars on their sides because of rough riders wearing spurs.

Whip or bat: Using a whip called a bat will give your legs extra power. If your horse is being lazy or ignoring your leg aids, use a bat. You may need one on the trail, for example, if your horse is stubborn about going into water or passing strange objects. You may also need one to discipline your horse if he displays aggression

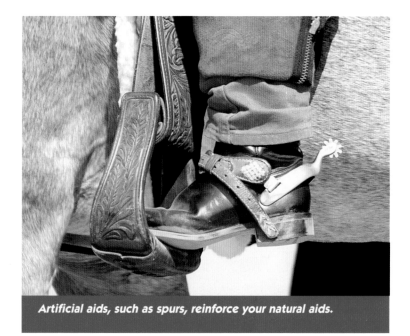

Artificial aids, such as spurs, reinforce your natural aids.

toward other horses. If he kicks another horse, you must smack him with the whip immediately.

Only use a whip behind your leg, on your horse's sides. Give him one or two smart smacks and then continue with your work. Don't hold on to the reins tightly and whack your horse with the same hand because the rein will yank him in the mouth.

Never lose your temper and beat your horse with a whip, and never use one around his head. It will frighten him and make him "head shy"—afraid of having his head touched.

Reins: Occasionally you can use a romal or the ends of your reins to reinforce your leg aids.

If your horse ignores you, snap the romal or reins against his side. He should react quickly. Using your reins like this should be a last resort because it doesn't look very stylish, and you could jerk on his mouth in the process.

You may need to snap the ends of your reins to get a slow horse to move forward.

First Steps

Once you've mounted, check your position before you set off at the walk. Are your legs in the right position? Are you sitting up straight? Do you feel comfortable and relaxed in the saddle?

When you're ready, look straight ahead. Nudge the horse's barrel with your heels or squeeze him with your calves. When he walks forward, stop giving him the leg aid immediately. Reward him when he obeys you, and don't nag him by continually kicking or poking him with your legs.

Keep the insides of your calves touching your horse's sides while he's walking, but if he's obedient and forward-moving, you shouldn't have to keep squeezing. Concentrate on keeping your heels down and your toes pointing straight ahead or slightly out.

Most western horses are ridden on a loose rein, but this doesn't mean that you will ride with no control. Maintain a light contact on

Look straight ahead when walking.

the reins, not too loose and not too tight. Don't hang on your horse's mouth. The reins should make a gentle arc from the bit to your hand, but you must be able to make contact with the horse's mouth quickly if you need to turn or halt him. If you hold the reins with one hand, keep the hand as steady as possible because it helps keep your horse balanced. If you hold the reins with two hands, keep them level and let them follow the bobbing movement of the horse's head.

Sometimes it's hard to keep a lazy horse moving. Should you kick him? Kicking can upset a horse and deaden his sides forever. And it makes you look like a bad, ineffective rider. If you get stuck on a slowpoke, use short, sharp squeezes from your lower legs to get him going. Once he's moving, reward him by leaving him alone. If he only pokes along, squeeze him with alternate legs to keep him going. Squeeze once with your left leg, then as he steps forward, squeeze with your right leg. Again, when you get the desired pace, stop squeezing.

When using both hands to rein, squeeze just one rein to ask your horse to turn.

If he still won't step out, strap on a pair of spurs, but use them sparingly. Nudge him once or twice with the spurs and the second he responds, remove them from his side.

Steering

Once your horse is walking, it won't be long before you have to turn him. When you're learning how to ride, it seems natural to pull on the reins to get your horse to move in the direction you want to go, but simply using the reins isn't the most effective way to turn a horse. You must use your legs to guide him too. Before you make

To neck rein, move your hand and both reins in the direction you want to go.

your turn, look in the direction you want to go, then ask your horse to turn. Here are the two ways most western riders hold the reins:

Holding the reins with two hands: You use a "leading" or "opening" rein when riding with two hands. This means you actually lead the horse's head by applying pressure to the rein closest to the direction you want to turn. A leading rein comes in handy when riding a green horse or a horse that wears a snaffle.

Ask your horse to turn left by moving your left hand about 3 or 4 inches away from his neck and squeezing on the rein. He should turn his head to the left, and you should be able to see his left eye. Keep your right hand close to his neck, and keep a steady but soft feel on the rein. If he doesn't turn right away, tug gently on the left rein several times to get his attention. Reward him when he turns by softening your hold on the left rein.

At the same time, keep your left leg near the cinch and move your right one back behind the cinch a couple inches. These are the aids that tell your horse to bend his body to the left. Your right leg, behind the cinch, tells him not to swing his hindquarters out and straighten up. Once the turn is complete, stop squeezing the left rein and move your right leg back to the cinch.

If you're turning your horse to the right, squeeze the right rein until he turns his head. Keep your right leg next to the cinch and your left leg slightly behind the cinch. When riding in a circle, remember "inside leg next to the cinch, outside leg behind the cinch" and you should be able to maintain your horse's bend nicely.

Holding both reins with one hand: Most western riders hold both reins in one hand, because of the tradition of needing the right hand for utility purposes. When riding with one hand, you must neck rein to steer your horse. Neck reining means that when you move your rein hand in the direction you want to go, to the left for example, the right rein puts pressure on the horse's neck and asks him to move away from it.

When your horse halts, his weight should be distributed evenly over his legs.

Once again, use your legs to help you steer. To turn to the right, press your left leg behind the cinch to push his hindquarters over and keep your right leg at the cinch to maintain his bend. Some horses are so experienced and well trained that they react quickly to the neck rein and barely need any leg pressure at all.

Turning Tips

Use your hands quietly when turning. Don't lift them in the air or yank your horse around with the reins. Your movements should be subtle. Rough hands can damage a horse's mouth, making him unresponsive and difficult to steer.

Don't lean in the direction you're turning or put too much weight in one stirrup because you will unbalance your horse and make the turn look and feel clumsy.

Halting

Prepare yourself to halt before giving your horse any cues. Sit deep on both of your seat bones in the middle of the saddle. Keep your back straight and look ahead to where you want to halt. To begin to halt, stop squeezing with your legs and simply let them rest against his sides.

If you're neck reining, say "whoa" slowly and apply pressure on the bit with your rein hand. This means squeezing with your fingers to lift the slack out of the reins. If your horse doesn't respond to such subtle cues, you may need to move your hand back slightly, toward your stomach. The second your horse halts, reward him by releasing the pressure on the reins.

In simple terms: let go of his mouth. If you're using two hands, say "whoa" and squeeze on both reins at the same time.

If your horse doesn't stop right away, don't pull until he halts. Most horses fight against a constant hold and pull against you. Small tugs or squeezes are usually more effective than constant pulling. Too often, people are rough with their hands when asking a horse to halt. Rough hands make a horse resist and throw his head in the air to avoid mouth pain.

Disobedient horses may pull against you no matter what you do. In this case, be more aggressive. Sit back in the saddle, lift your hand(s) up slightly, and give several quick pulls on the horse's mouth until he stops.

Once you can halt your horse, try to get him to "stand square." This means he halts with his two front legs and his two hind legs lined up evenly. His head, neck, and back should be straight and his weight should be distributed evenly on all four legs. If he doesn't stand square the first time, nudge him forward a step or two.

Practice halting frequently. Ask him to stand quietly when you chat to a friend or while you watch others ride. Some horses fidget and move around when asked to halt. If your horse won't stand quietly, ask him to halt for only a few seconds, then let him walk for-

Limber up by doing airplanes.

Leg crunches will strengthen your leg muscles.

ward. As his behavior improves, try to lengthen the time he stands still. Praise him and pat him on the neck when he halts nicely.

There may come a time when your horse must stand quietly. You have to line up and stand still at shows, and a judge will mark down a fidgety horse. You may also need to stop on a trail ride to let other horses or a car pass.

If your horse won't stand still, work on halting him from the ground. Lead him around in his bridle and ask him to stop and stand still. Say "whoa" or "ho" and tug on the reins to make him halt.

Exercises and Stretches You Can Do in the Saddle

Now that you can control your horse, try some easy exercises in the saddle. They're a great way to work on your position, limber you up, make you feel more comfortable on your horse, and help improve your balance. You can do exercises at the walk or jog, and you might find them easier at first if your horse is on a lunge line. Make sure you do these exercises on a calm, obedient horse:

Toe Touches: Hold the reins in your left hand, and with your right hand, reach over the horse's neck and touch your left toe. Repeat with the other hand and opposite leg.

Airplanes: Hold the reins in one hand and stretch out your other arm horizontally. Make five big circles with the arm, then switch the reins and repeat with the other arm. If you're on a lunge line, circle both arms at the same time.

Forward Stretches: Lean forward and touch your horse's poll with both hands. Try to keep your lower legs in the correct position close to the cinch. Now lean back and touch his dock.

Leg Lifts: Take both of your feet out of the stirrups and slowly lift your legs up and away from the saddle. Hold them up for a couple of seconds, then lower them slowly back into position at your horse's sides.

Leg Crunches: Take one foot out of the stirrup and lift it up and toward the back so you can grab your calf or ankle with your hand. Bend at the knee until you can feel the front of your thigh muscles flexing.

The Jog

Once you're able to walk, turn, and stop your horse, you can move up a gear to the jog, which is a slow trot. You'll find this gait is slightly bumpier than the nice, smooth walk. The first time you jog, you'll probably bounce around a bit. Hang on to the horn at first, because you want to keep a fairly loose rein so you don't yank your horse in the mouth.

One of the best ways to learn to jog is on a lunge line. If you take lessons, ask your trainer to lunge your horse while you get used to the bumpy motion. You'll be able to concentrate on keeping your balance without worrying about what the horse is doing. Some horses are bumpier than others, and you may find staying secure in the saddle requires a lot of effort. You'll be using muscles you haven't used before, so ride at the jog for only a few minutes at a time. Your position at the jog should be the same as it is at the walk:

- Look in the direction you're going.
- Keep your elbows close to your body.
- Sit up tall and keep your back straight.
- Sit deep in the saddle and distribute your weight evenly on both seat bones.
- Keep your lower legs close to your horse's sides.

To pick up the jog, squeeze your horse's sides with your lower legs. If she doesn't respond, squeeze again and again, or give her a nudge with your heels. If she still won't move out, tap her behind your leg with a whip, or snap the ends of the reins on her flank.

Relax so you can absorb the horse's jogging motion.

The jog has a definite rhythm, and you must develop a feel for it. It's known as a two-beat gait. You should be able to feel a "one-two, one-two, one-two" beat. Counting this beat out loud may help you get in sync with your horse's motion.

While jogging, keep your legs on your horse's sides. You may need to nudge her occasionally with your heels to keep her moving forward. Your thighs should touch the saddle. If you're reining with one hand, hold your hand steady over the horn and keep a soft, but constant feel on your horse's mouth. If you're reining with two hands, keep them soft and flexible to follow the nodding movement of your horse's head. Avoid pulling on your horse's mouth.

Try to relax and absorb the jogging motion with your whole body. Keep your rear end as close to the saddle seat as possible and let your hips move with the horse. If, at first, you feel as if you're going to bounce right out of the saddle, stand up in your stirrups for a few seconds to regain your balance. Hold on to the saddle horn if you need to, but don't make it a habit.

Posting (Rising) Trot

You may be asked to trot in a show class, or you may trot on a trail if you're in a hurry to get somewhere. When a horse trots, she springs from one diagonal pair of legs to the other. For example, her front right leg and her back left leg move forward at the same time. Then the front left leg and back right leg move forward together. There is a moment of suspension in the air between each step, which is why the trot feels so bouncy.

Because the trot is faster and bumpier than the jog, it's more tiring because you're absorbing the horse's up-and-down motion. Posting lessens the stress on you and your horse. When posting, you rise out of the saddle when one diagonal pair of legs springs off the ground, and sit down as the same pair returns to the ground. You'll notice that the natural movement of your horse's gait bounces you forward and slightly out of the saddle, making

When you trot it may be easier to post (rise) out of the saddle.

posting happen almost naturally. When learning how to post, count "one-two, one-two, one-two" until you start to feel a rhythm, then rise on "one" and sit on "two." You can post on trail rides or while you work in the ring, but generally it's not allowed in western classes in which you're being judged.

Diagonals

Learning how to post is essential before you begin the process of learning diagonals, so be sure you feel your posting skills are strong before proceeding.

Once you are comfortable posting, you must master diagonals—a simple way of making sure you're up out of the saddle or sitting down in the saddle on the correct beat. Tradition dictates that the diagonal you should be on depends on the direction your horse is traveling in an arena. If you're riding around the ring to

Sit down when your horse's outside leg is underneath her.

the right (your right hand is closest to the center of the arena), rise and sit in time with your horse's left foreleg (the one closest to the fence of the arena). When riding to the left, rise and sit in time with your horse's right foreleg.

How do you check if you're on the correct diagonal? Sneak a peek at your horse's outside leg as you are practicing. When the leg is forward, you should be up in the air. When the leg is back under your horse, you should be sitting in the saddle.

If you change direction, you must change your diagonal to correspond. To do this, simply sit in the saddle for two beats, then rise again. Think to yourself: up-down, up-down, down-up. If you're still on the wrong diagonal, sit down another two beats, then rise.

Out on a trail, where there is no inside or outside rail, change your diagonal every once in a while. This will keep your horse flexible—she won't get used to being on one diagonal.

Don't tilt your head down when checking your diagonal.

Transitions

You have to make a transition going from the walk to the jog. A transition is the way to change gaits; for example, from walk to jog or jog to lope. An upward transition means going from a slower gait to a faster gait. A downward transition means going from a faster gait to a slower gait.

Your goal as an efficient rider is to make transitions as smoothly as possible. When you ask your horse to jog, it shouldn't take two minutes of kicking to get her to react. And when you ask for the walk from the jog, you shouldn't have to pull and pull on the reins to get her to slow down. A downward transition should take only a few steps.

If your horse is well-balanced and paying attention to you when you ask for a transition, it shouldn't be too hard for her to speed up or slow down smoothly and without a fuss. But if she's slopping along with her nose on the ground, or high-stepping it with her head in the air, your transitions will be messy. Settle your horse before you ask for a transition if you want a successful change.

Ask for upward transitions by squeezing or nudging your horse with your legs or heels. Loosen your hold on the reins so you don't yank her mouth when she shifts up a gear. When you ask for a downward transition, sit deep in the saddle and push your shoulders back. Keep your legs on your horse's sides, but don't kick or squeeze. Put pressure on the reins with your fingers, or move your hand back slightly so you can feel her mouth. The instant your horse slows down, loosen your hold on her mouth as a reward.

Jogging Exercises

Here are some easy-to-remember exercises for you to do while working your horse in the ring:

Circles: Do a lot of circles at the jog. Circles make your horse more supple. Do small ones and big ones, and keep them round, not misshapen. Try to keep your horse's body bent around your inside leg. You should be able to see her inside eye when you're circling.

Changes of Direction: Change your direction frequently so you don't bore your horse. Ride down the center of the arena or cut across the middle.

Transitions: Go from walk to jog, jog to walk, jog to halt, etc. Doing plenty of transitions keeps your horse alert and thinking.

When circling, bend your horse's body around your inside leg.

Serpentines: Practice making large S-shaped figures up and down the arena. Keep your loops even.

Figure Eights: Practice figure eights at the walk, jog, and trot. Both circles should be round-shaped and the same size. If you're posting in a figure eight, remember to change your diagonal when you change directions in the middle of the eight.

Leg Yielding: Leg yielding produces a sideways movement in which your horse moves away from your leg pressure. Try it on the long side of the arena. Make sure your horse's body is straight as you walk or jog. Put your outside leg slightly behind the cinch, while the inside leg stays at the cinch. Then press your horse's side with your outside leg, which asks her to move her haunches away from the pressure. Use your inside leg to keep the shoulders from falling out and to keep her walking. She should move forward and sideways at the same time. Even pressure with your reins should keep her going straight, not crooked. After she moves sideways for a few steps, let her go straight for a second or two, then use your other leg to ask her to move back to the track again.

Praise and Rewards

Always remember to praise your horse while working her. Positive reinforcement can work wonders for the horse. If she performs a movement well, pat or stroke her neck with your hand and praise her verbally. Say "good girl" in a soothing, pleasant tone. Horses know the difference between praise and correction. Reward your horse by letting her relax occasionally. Loosen your hold on the reins and let her walk at her own pace for a moment or two.

If your horse is acting up, correct her quickly. If she's being lazy or stubborn, tap her with the crop to get her moving. If she ignores your instructions or is being naughty, sometimes a growl or a sharp verbal "No!" can make a horse focus on her work.

Never lose your temper, and don't hit your horse unless she has done something really bad, such as kicking or biting another horse. Even then, one or two hard smacks on her rump and a "no" should be enough. Always discipline your horse immediately if she displays dangerous behavior. Don't wait, because seconds later she won't remember why she is being punished because a horse's attention span is rather short. You basically have three seconds to mete out a correction if you want the horse to be able to associate the bad behavior with the consequences, so act swiftly and firmly remembering all the while to treat your horse humanely.

Reward your horse's good behavior with a pat.

Riding Bareback

Many trainers believe that riding bareback can help you develop a secure seat. In fact, many of them start their students bareback. Without the help of the saddle and horn, you must rely on your natural sense of balance or develop it pretty quickly! If you find riding without a saddle a bit slippery or uncomfortable, try using a bareback pad. This is a thick saddle pad with a girth for extra security.

It's a good idea to stay in an arena when you first ride bareback because if you take a dive, your horse can't go far! Use a

Use a bareback pad if your horse is uncomfortable to ride without a saddle.

Riding a bareback horse can help develop a secure seat.

mounting block, rock, or nearby fence to mount your horse. Once you're seated, sit up straight and let your legs hang down next to your horse's sides. Your thighs should rest on your horse, and your lower legs should lightly touch her. Sit evenly on both seat bones and try to relax. Hold your hands as you would when riding with a saddle.

Ask your horse to walk forward the same way you would normally ask her (by squeezing her with your calves). Riding bareback at the walk is pretty easy; it's the jog that can be tough! When jogging, try to relax and absorb the bumpy movement in your thighs and seat. Move with the horse as much as you can, and keep your legs long and around your horse's barrel. Don't grip with your thighs or knees, and don't pull your legs up. This just makes you stiff, and you bounce even more.

The Lope and the Gallop

Once you feel secure in the saddle at the jog and trot, you can try loping. The lope is a smoother pace than the jog and can be very comfortable. It is known as a three-beat gait. When your horse lopes while on the right lead, his hooves move in this sequence: left hind lands and pushes the horse forward; the right hind and left fore land at the same time; and then the leading right fore hits the ground. There is a moment of suspension in the air until the left hind lands again. This makes your horse rock back and forth, which makes you rock back and forth too.

The lope is faster than the jog, so you need to be in complete control of your horse before you ask him to go faster. It's a good idea to learn how to lope in an enclosed arena, instead of out on a trail or in a big field so your horse doesn't take advantage and run off with you.

When you're first learning to lope, you'll probably ask for it from the jog. Experienced horses can pick up the lope from the walk, but it's easier for them to start from the jog. It is easier for you as well, because your horse should already be moving forward at the pace needed to pick up the lope.

Before you ask your horse to lope, make sure you're sitting correctly. Sit deep in the saddle, and ask your horse to slow down to a smooth, evenly paced jog. Concentrate on keeping your back straight, and look ahead. Make sure your reins are even on both sides of your horse's neck, and keep your legs on his sides.

Ride in the safe confines of an arena when first loping.

Leads

Plan to pick up the lope as your horse jogs in a circle or around a bend in the arena. If he begins loping on a curve, he is more likely to pick up the correct lead. When your horse lopes, his inside foreleg should reach farther forward and step a bit higher than his outside foreleg.

The inside leg is sometimes called the "leading leg" by trainers. Your horse will be better balanced if he is on the correct lead. When you compete in western riding classes, the judge expects you to be on the correct lead when he asks for the lope. This is why it's important to learn the cues that tell your horse to take off on the correct lead. If you have to return to the jog to pick up the correct lead, you will probably not get a ribbon in your class.

If you're having a hard time getting your horse to pick up the correct lead, lunge him without a rider for a few days. If he

Ask for the lope while jogging in a circle to help your horse start on the correct lead.

At the lope, your horse's inside foreleg should reach farther than his outside foreleg.

If you can't get your horse on the correct lead, lunge him without a rider at the lope to see if the problem is rider-related.

has problems picking up the lead on the lunge line, he may have back or leg problems that are affecting his performance and overall health. If you suspect that your horse is uncomfortable, call the veterinarian for an evaluation.

If your horse picks up the lead easily on the lunge line, his rider (that's you) is probably the problem. If your position is not correct or you don't know how to cue your horse the right way, your horse may have difficulty getting balanced enough to pick up the correct lead or he may not understand what you are asking. Maybe you need to sign up for some sessions with a reputable trainer to get a better handle on the challenge of leading. The extra time and money can pay off in the long run. Explain your problem, and let the trainer ride your horse and watch you and your horse in action. He may be able to suggest some training exercises to solve your lead problems; and he may also work on your position in the saddle.

Asking for the Lope

When you reach the arena corner or while you're circling, ask your horse to bend around your inside leg. Place your inside leg next to the cinch and your outside leg slightly behind the cinch. If you're using two reins, squeeze the inside rein so your horse turns his head inward. If you're neck reining, move your hand over toward the inside so the pressure of the rein makes him turn his head toward the middle of the arena. You want to see your horse's inside eye.

When your horse is bending properly and feels balanced, ask for the lope. If he is moping along with his head toward the ground—or speeding along with his nose in the air—it's likely he'll take off on the wrong lead. Once your horse is moving forward nicely at the jog, give him the following cues to ask him to lope:

- Sit on both seat bones in the saddle.
- Push your heels down and point your toes forward.
- Slightly shift your weight to the outside seat bone. It's easier for the horse to pick up the inside lead if your body is not leaning to the inside. This weight shift should be invisible. People watching should not be able to tell that you have shifted your weight.
- Keep your inside leg near the cinch, and with your calf, give your horse a squeeze, or with your outside leg behind the cinch, give a nudge. Some riders also cluck or make a kissing sound to tell their horses, usually experienced mounts, to begin loping.

If your horse doesn't strike off immediately, maintain his bend and nudge him harder with your outside leg. If he still ignores you, use a crop behind your outside leg or touch him with the spur on your outside leg. If a horse ignores your natural aids, it's better to use the artificial ones immediately, rather than continue kicking.

When your horse does strike off, it feels as if he's leaping forward. Try to relax and follow your horse's rocking movement with your hips. Press your rear end into the saddle and keep your legs firmly in place. This may seem difficult at first because your legs may swing with the horse's movement. Try pushing your heels down and putting more weight in your stirrups. It may also help to squeeze lightly with your legs every time his inside foreleg reaches back and then loosen your legs when his inside foreleg reaches forward. Touching your horse lightly with your lower leg during each stride helps both of you stay more balanced. If all else fails, hold onto the cantle, the back of the saddle seat.

If you're riding with two reins, keep your hands soft and the reins long enough that you can follow the motion of the horse's head and neck but short enough so you can stop him quickly and easily. If you're neck reining with one hand, keep a light contact on his mouth and keep your hand steady above his neck. It's important that you don't yank him in the mouth every time he surges forward. You want your horse to feel that he can move forward freely.

Some horses, especially green ones, tend to lurch forward into the lope at top speed, and while they're zipping along you may have a tough time getting them balanced. If your horse does this, let him continue for a stride or two before you bring him back by sitting deep in the saddle and putting pressure on the reins. The second he slows down, loosen your hold on the reins as a reward.

When you start riding, you may not be able to tell if your horse is on the correct lead simply by "feel." You may have to look down to make sure his inside leg is stretching out farther than his outside hoof. Try not to tip your whole head down, though, because this can unbalance you and your horse. Simply look down with your eyes. As you become more experienced, you'll be able to tell right away that your horse isn't on the correct lead. When they lope on the wrong lead, most horses feel unbalanced, stiff, and awkward.

Looking down to check the lead can affect your balance.

If your horse strikes off on the wrong lead, bring him back to the jog immediately. Jog a few steps until you feel that both of you are well balanced, then ask for the lope again. Sit deep in the saddle, turn your horse's head to the inside, and with your outside leg behind the cinch, give him a nudge. If your horse is not balanced when you ask him to "shift gears," he may take off into a "disunited lope"—also known as "cross-firing." This means that when you're riding to the right, he may lead with his left front and his right hind instead of the left hind. You'll know if he is doing this because riding him will be pretty bumpy. Slow him down to the jog and cue him to lope again.

Loping Tips

- Don't lean to the inside when asking for the lope. This unbalances your horse and makes him likely to strike off on the wrong leg. Sit in the middle of the saddle, stay centered on his back, and lean slightly to the outside.
- If you get left behind in the rocking motion, adjust your position quickly. Sitting too far back will make your legs fly forward and you won't feel secure in the saddle. Leaning too far forward tells your horse to speed up, and you don't want that right now.
- Make sure you lope equally on both leads. Many horses pick up one lead better than the other, so it's important to work your horse in both directions during your training and exercise sessions.

Loping Exercises

Circles

Do plenty of circles at the lope. Circles help your horse become more supple. Include some increasing and decreasing circles. Work your horse in a small 10-meter circle, then gradually increase the size to 20 meters, then decrease the circle again.

Transitions

Once your horse is fairly balanced, you can ask him to do some more advanced transitions. Instead of slowing down from a lope to a jog, ask your horse to halt from the lope. You can also ask him to lope from the walk instead of the jog. Your goal is to have your horse make these transitions smoothly and not make a fuss when you ask him to do something a little bit different. Just make sure your cues are correct and efficient. Think about how you're going to ask your horse to change his pace before you actually do it.

Many well-trained horses can change leads in midair.

Figure Eights and Flying Lead Changes

Do large figure eights with a straight center line between the two loops. Lope in a circle in one direction, then bring your horse back to the jog in the middle of the eight on the straightaway. Once he's jogging, ask for the lope on the other leading leg and head in the other direction. This is called a simple lead change because you bring the horse back to the jog before striking off on the other lead.

As you and your horse become more proficient about picking up the correct lead, you can attempt flying lead changes in the middle of the eight when you change direction. A flying lead change is when a horse changes leading legs while he is loping.

Your horse has to know how to do flying lead changes if you intend to show him in reining classes. Almost every reining test includes at least one change of lead, and you will be marked down if you slow your horse to a jog to switch leads. The judge may also ask for flying lead changes in western riding and horsemanship classes.

A series of figure eights is one way to teach your horse how to do them. Start by loping on one lead. Come back to the jog in the middle of the eight and ask for the different leading leg with your normal loping cues: outside leg behind the cinch, inside leg near the cinch. Start decreasing the time you allow your horse to jog. Give him only a stride or two to change leads. Finally, stop asking for the jog. In the middle of the figure eight, if your horse is traveling to the right, give him the cues that you would give him if you were asking him to lope to the left. If you're riding with two reins, raise the left rein slightly so he turns his head, shift your right seat bone subtly to the right, keep your left leg next to the cinch, and give him a strong nudge behind the cinch with your right leg. If you're riding with one hand, move your rein hand slightly upward and to the left. If he switches in midair, continue cantering around on the left and then let him stop and have a break. Flying lead changes can be hard for a green horse, so take it easy at first.

Lean slightly forward when galloping.

The Gallop

The gallop is the horse's fastest speed, and for most riders it's the most exciting gait to ride. It is faster than the lope because the horse takes bigger strides.

Galloping is a lot of fun, but it can be dangerous. It is very easy for a horse speeding along at full speed to get out of control, especially if he's being ridden by an inexperienced rider. It's also easy for him to stumble, causing his rider to fall. Practice galloping in an enclosed arena before you try it on the trail. It is important you can stop or slow down your horse at all times before you attempt to gallop.

Preparing to Gallop

Once your horse is loping, hold your rein hand or reins on the upper part of your horse's neck, lean your upper body forward a little, lift your rear slightly out of the saddle, and squeeze strongly with your legs. Your horse can go even faster when you sit like this because your weight is off his hindquarters and he can use them more efficiently and comfortably. Continue squeezing until your horse goes faster.

Keep your hand up his neck so the reins are fairly slack. You don't want to yank your horse in the mouth when he stretches out his neck. Once your horse is galloping, squeeze your legs in rhythm with his galloping stride. Look straight ahead to make sure the path ahead is clear.

When you want your horse to slow down, stop squeezing with your legs and sit down quietly in the saddle. If your horse understands voice commands, say "whoa" slowly. If he doesn't stop, pick up the slack in your reins. If you're holding the reins with one hand, pull it back and put some pressure on his mouth. If you are riding with two reins, take up the slack and squeeze on both reins. If your horse still won't slow down, circle him. Make the circles smaller and smaller until he finds it difficult to continue galloping.

6

Horse Problems

If you're taking riding lessons, you'll soon discover that not all horses behave perfectly. Some are easy to ride. They are obedient and obey your cues. But others ignore your signals and do exactly as they please—especially if you're new to riding.

Just like people, horses have a bad habit or two. Some equine habits such as sneaking a mouthful of grass aren't serious. Others such as bucking, bolting, or rearing are dangerous and could injure you, your horse, or other people.

If your horse is normally a happy camper but suddenly develops a disturbing behavior—don't panic. You might be able to solve the problem yourself without much help. First, figure out why your horse is acting the way she is, then try to alter her behavior.

Reasons for Bad Behavior

Here are a few reasons your horse may suddenly start behaving badly:

Too much feed and too little work: If your horse is fed too much high-energy feed and doesn't do enough work, you're asking for trouble. Your horse will be frisky, full of herself, and have plenty of energy for obnoxious activities such as bucking and bolting. If your horse is acting overly rambunctious, start by giving her a low-energy feed. Low energy feeds have no oats, which can make a horse "hot" (excitable). You should also cut down on her concentrates such as sweet feed and replace them with low-energy

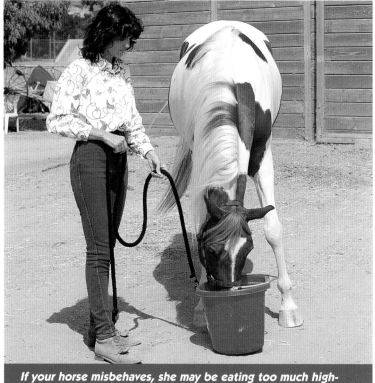

If your horse misbehaves, she may be eating too much high-energy food.

roughage such as hay. If you're feeding your horse an extra-rich hay such as alfalfa, consider switching her to low-energy orchard grass hay.

If your horse is too hot, let her spend a lot of time in a field or turn-out area to get rid of excess energy by running around and exercising herself. You can also lunge her for about fifteen minutes before you ride, but it is better simply to adjust her feed.

Her tack doesn't fit correctly: If your horse's tack doesn't fit her properly, it could hurt her and make her uncomfortable when you ride. She may not be able to concentrate on her work. She may

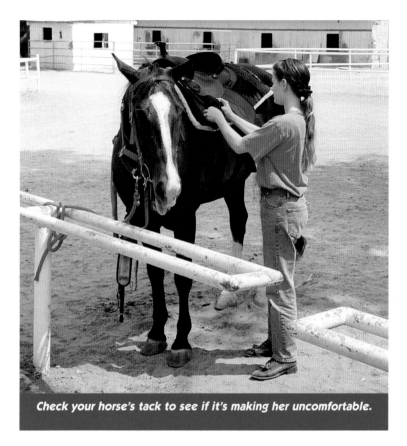

Check your horse's tack to see if it's making her uncomfortable.

buck or bolt to avoid the pain. If your saddle blanket is lumpy in places, it could hurt her back. If your saddletree is too narrow, it will pinch her withers. If her bit is too low in her mouth, it could bang her teeth and upset her.

Check your tack thoroughly to make sure it fits your horse. If it doesn't, have it adjusted by a saddler or buy new tack. Your horse's comfort—and, ultimately, your safety—is worth the effort and expense.

She is sick: A horse not feeling up to par may be unwilling to do her normal work. She may be sluggish and stubborn—for exam-

Are you really a good enough rider for your horse?

If you're having problems with your horse, sign up for lessons with a reputable trainer.

ple, unresponsive to cues and/or tossing her head—and if this unusual behavior lasts for more than a day or two, ask your vet to give your horse a checkup. A sore leg or aching tooth can make a horse miserable.

Rider problems: Poor riding can make a horse act up. If you're bouncing up and down in the saddle and yanking on your horse's mouth with rough reins, she's bound to become irritable and unwilling to work. She may buck or rear to escape your heavy-handed riding, and who can blame her? If you're having a lot of problems with your horse, you may need to think critically about your riding skills. Are you a good enough rider for this particular horse? (Some horses are more forgiving than others.) If you feel you're not clicking with your horse, sign up for lessons with a qualified instructor. An instructor may be able to pinpoint some position problems that are hindering your horse's performance. It may be discouraging to watch a professional mount your horse and ride her better than you can, but if the trainer is worth his or her salt, he or she knows the goal is to help you ride your horse effectively.

Don't feel bad about seeking professional help for your horse. It is more important that you get some help before the serious control problems get worse—and they will. Find a trainer you trust, and describe your horse's behavior to her. The trainer will want to spend some time watching you and your horse together and may give you a few lessons from the ground. She may be able to devise a plan of action or come up with some solutions you haven't considered.

A trainer may want to ride your horse for a few weeks, or even months, to see if she can solve the problems. Be prepared to move your horse to the trainer's barn, but think twice before sending your horse off to a trainer to be "fixed." Don't expect your horse to be perfect four weeks later. The problems may return when you start riding her again. It's better to work with your trainer to solve a problem. You need to ride your horse on a regular basis too. If you're nervous about the horse's problem, ride only when your trainer is around. If you do move your horse to your trainer's barn, make sure that you arrange for regular lessons, and that you can stop by and visit the horse at any time. A reputable trainer should not mind your dropping by to watch her work with your horse and should be happy to show you her training methods.

If your horse is too much for you to handle and you're not having any fun, you must consider selling her. There is probably someone out there who can handle her and will enjoy her. Try to sell her privately, or ask your trainer to sell her. It is often easier to let a trainer work with a difficult horse for a while and sell her for you.

Let go of the reins if you fall.

Falling Off

Everyone falls off, even the most experienced riders, so keep your spirits up and keep trying. When you first learn to ride, you aren't very balanced and may fall off once in a while, but as you become better, you'll find that you're more secure in the saddle. You'll learn how to anticipate what your horse is going to do and prepare for it and react to it like a pro. The more experienced you become, the more confident you become and the less likely you are to eat dirt!

There are many reasons for falling off, including:

- You're a new rider and are not secure in the saddle.
- Your horse spooks at something and unbalances you.
- Your horse misbehaves and bucks you off.
- Your tack is in bad shape and breaks while you're riding. (Clean and check your tack regularly.)

If you think you're about to fall off your horse, you may have to take desperate measures to stay in the saddle. Hang on to the horn, or lean down as close as you can to your horse's neck and wrap your arms around her. This isn't the time to worry about your position. If you fall off, here's what you should do to try to prevent serious injury:

1. Let go of the reins. If you hang on to the reins, you will be dragged along behind your horse and she could kick you. It's better to have broken reins than broken arms.

2. Curl up. Bring your arms close to your body and curl up into a ball. Don't hold your arms out to break your fall. You'll only break your arms.

3. Lie still. Once you hit the ground, lie still for a moment. You may feel dizzy, especially if you've hit your head. Sit up slowly. If you're in pain, yell for help. If you can, stand up slowly. If your horse hasn't galloped back to the barn and you're not injured, it's a tremendous confidence builder to remount and get back to work.

In the aftermath, try not to think too much about the fall. You may not be as confident for a while. This is natural. Stick to the ring or familiar trails until you get your nerve back. You will soon put the fall behind you and become a more self-confident and experienced rider because of it.

Bucking

When a horse bucks, she puts her head down, arches her back, and kicks her hind legs in the air. This may happen if her saddle or cinch is pinching her or if she has too much energy and is simply feeling good. Some badly behaved horses buck to remove pesky riders. If your horse bucks a lot, check her tack to make sure it fits properly.

If your horse puts her head down and you think she's going to buck, pull her head up as quickly as you can. Tug on the reins and kick her so she moves forward. It's difficult for a horse to buck if she's moving forward. Sit deep in the saddle and lean backward. It's best to ignore this behavior and keep her working hard. If you make a big deal out of bucking, she may do it more.

Bolting

When you lose control and a horse gallops off with you it's called bolting. A horse may bolt because she is overly excited or scared of something. When she bolts, she doesn't always look where she's going and could knock people or other horses over. Bolting can be terrifying, but you must stay calm and stop the horse quickly. Use the pulley rein technique to stop a bolting horse. Here's how:

1. Sit deep in the saddle.

2. Shorten your hold on the reins considerably.

3. Keep one hand and rein close to the withers, and with the other hand, pull back sharply. Pull until she turns her head toward you. If she doesn't turn her head, try the other hand and rein.

4. Circle! Circle! Circle! It's almost impossible for a horse to continue galloping while running in a tight circle. Make the circle smaller and smaller until she slows down.

Rearing

A horse standing up on her hind legs might be impressive in an old western movie, but it's very dangerous and you could get hurt. If your horse is a chronic rearer, this is not the horse for you.

A horse may rear because she doesn't want to move forward. She may also rear if she's upset or confused. Unfortunately, once she learns that rearing is an effective way of avoiding work, she'll do it again and again.

Never pull back on the reins if your horse rears. You'll unbalance her, and she could fall over backward on top of you. If you think she's going to rear, turn her quickly or kick her so she moves forward. Use a crop if you have to.

She can't rear if she is moving forward. If she does, loosen your hold on the reins, lean forward, and wrap your arms around her neck. When she lands, kick her or spur her so she moves forward immediately.

Grass Grabbing

Most horses act as if they're starving all the time. When they spot a tasty bit of grass they lunge for it, whether or not they have riders on their backs. Some horses think of trails as one big salad bar. They put their heads down and munch every chance they get. Don't be a softy. If you let your horse grab grass whenever she wants, she'll do it all the time. When riding, keep your horse's head up and maintain a hold on the reins. She can eat on her own time.

If your grass grabber is ridden by a child or an inexperienced rider, put grass reins on the horse to stop her munching. Simply tie a long piece of twine to each bit ring, or if you are using a curb bit,

For some horses, the world is a salad bar! Maintain a hold on the reins to prevent grass grabbing.

Grass reins will stop a horse from grabbing grass.

tie the twine to the ring at the top of the bit cheek. Then run the twine up alongside the cheekpiece and through the browband loop. Finally, tie the twine to the breastplate rings on either side of the front of the saddle. The twine should be short enough to prevent your horse from lowering her head to graze but long enough so she can bob her head freely when she moves.

Kicking

If you have a horse who kicks other horses, alert anyone who rides near you. Once warned, it's the other rider's responsibility to

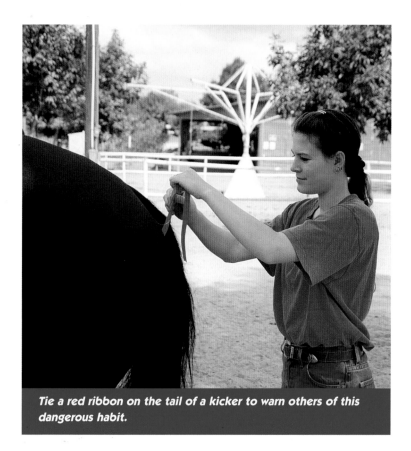

Tie a red ribbon on the tail of a kicker to warn others of this dangerous habit.

give your horse plenty of room. Try your best to stay away from other horses, and if you're trail riding, stay at the back of the line. If you go to a show, tie a red ribbon on your horse's tail. This lets others know your horse kicks.

When your horse lifts her leg or acts aggressively toward another horse, give her a hard whack behind your leg with a crop and say "No!" in a firm voice. Then ask her to move forward. If she's working hard and listening to your cues, she shouldn't have time to think about kicking.

Trail Riding

As you become a more experienced rider, you'll soon realize there's more to riding than endlessly working your horse in the arena. It won't be long before you'll want to hit the trail with your horse. There's nothing like it. Riding in the countryside across large open fields, down woodsy trails, or up mountain paths is exhilarating, and your horse will enjoy it as much as you do. It's great exercise for him too. Climbing up and down hills builds muscles and stamina, and finding his way across unpredictable paths encourages independent thinking and teaches him to be alert. Trail riding also gives your horse a much-needed break from his arena workouts. Try to trail ride as much as possible. Consider your time in the open a mental-health break for both of you and have some fun.

Finding Trails

If you keep your horse at a boarding facility, ask other riders if they go on trail rides, if there are trails near your barn, and what sort of countryside the trails wind through. Maybe someone will volunteer to show you some of the nearby trails, or you can ask to join a group ride. In some areas, a trail organization or the local authorities maintain trails and you may be able to get a map of the local routes. If local authorities support the trails, other people have permission to use them too, so you may come across joggers, bicyclists, children, and hikers with dogs on these paths.

Take your horse camping at a state park.

Trail Etiquette

Not everyone knows how to act around horses. Be alert, but treat other trail users with the courtesy you expect to get in return. Their taxes help keep trails open, just as yours do. Slow down or halt to let joggers pass. Say "hello" and be friendly. If you see bicyclists, move over and let them pass. In return, mountain bikers should slow down or dismount while passing you, although they may not know this is the correct protocol around prey animals. Many horses are frightened of bicycles and you may need to wave to bicyclists and ask them politely to slow down. You may also have to ask adults to leash their dogs. Most will do as you ask if they realize they're upsetting your horse.

If you live in an urban area with no trails, find out if there are any state parks nearby that have riding trails. You may be able to trailer your horse there for a day. Some parks have lovely, well-groomed trails and areas where you can put your horse in a corral while you stop and have a picnic. You may even be able to put up a tent and spend the night. Find out if there are any other enthusiastic trail riders at your facility and arrange outings with them. You can also look in local horse magazines for resorts where you and your friends can take your horses for a couple of days and explore totally new surroundings.

Training Your Horse for the Trail

Not every horse is born trail-wise. It takes time and plenty of practice on the trail before your horse is completely comfortable in

Practice opening and shutting gates with your horse.

Get your horse used to standing quietly.

Walk your horse around his barn area so he gets used to the hustle and bustle of people.

the wilderness, however, there are ways to get him used to trail riding before you even leave the barn. On the trail you may come across a log or two that you want your horse to step over without a fuss, so put poles on the ground in the arena and incorporate them into your workout. Walk over them slowly. If he wants to jog or gets excited, slow him down and walk over the poles again and again until he steps over them calmly.

Practice halting and standing with a loose rein in the arena. Your horse shouldn't fidget; he should stand quietly and be relaxed. Let him relax and remain standing for up to five minutes. (You can chat to a friend.) Your horse needs to learn patience. He may have to stand completely still on a trail—for example, if a rattlesnake is crossing your path.

Open and shut the arena gate without dismounting. Walk up and position your horse parallel to the gate, with his head near the latch. Then reach down and pull the gate open. Use the leg closest to the gate to push your horse away from the gate. Ask your horse to halt next to the gate and stand quietly as you reach down to close it. A really clever horse learns how to push the gate shut with his chest, which comes in handy on the trail.

Your horse must get used to having horses in front of him and behind him. If your horse is fairly well behaved and doesn't kick, ask a friend to walk his horse right next to you in the ring, with very little room in between. Your horse needs to get used to being in close quarters with other horses before he hits the trails.

After your workout, stay on your horse and walk him around the barn area. This is a great way to get him used to dogs, cars, and other things that your horse finds frightening (such as garbage cans). Humans scuttling around and making noise shouldn't bother him much either, after a while.

First Trail

Before you head for the wilderness, you must have full control of your horse. Even the quietest animal can get excited in the open, and some horses may buck or bolt. You must be able to slow down your horse and bring him to a halt, and you must also be able to mount your horse from the ground. You never know when you might need to dismount on the trail, and there won't always be a rock or log handy.

It's best to go on your (or your horse's) first trail ride with an experienced trail-riding buddy who has a calm, sensible horse. Don't go out in a large crowd—this is guaranteed to excite or rattle your horse. You want your first trail ride to be a fairly sedate

Ride with a friend when you go on a trail ride.

experience. Ride with someone who understands this and doesn't want to gallop all over the place. Stick to a slow pace at first.

Follow your friend at first. Your horse should be happy to go behind. If he jogs or acts up, circle him and continually ask him to walk (by squeezing or pulling back on the reins lightly and sitting deep in the saddle). If your horse is behaving himself, walk alongside your friend. After a while, take the lead and see how your horse reacts. Alternate your position on the ride so your horse gets used to going in front and behind. There is nothing more annoying than a horse that won't follow quietly. Start your horse off right on his very first trail ride.

If your horse is a timid soul, going out with another more experienced horse is the best thing for him. If he's frightened of water, for example, he may follow his trail mate through it without a fuss. Other spooky objects, such as tractors or cows, will not scare him so much if his companion ignores them. Another good reason for going out with a pal is that if you fall off or get injured, your friend can fetch help. It's a smart idea to always ride with a friend.

Your Position in the Saddle

Part of the fun of trail riding is admiring the scenery, yet you still must pay attention to what is going on around you. Your horse could trip or spook and cause you to fall. You may be having a nice, relaxing time chatting with your friends, but it's essential you maintain a good riding position.

Your position on a trail ride should be much as it is in the arena. Keep your rear end firmly in the saddle and your legs on your horse's sides. Stay relaxed (this should be easy if your horse is behaving himself!) and move with your horse's forward motion. Maintain a fairly light contact on the reins so your horse can carry his neck and head naturally. You want to be able to pick up the reins quickly to stop him, but you also want to allow him some freedom of movement. The ground may be uneven on a trail and your horse may stumble or put his head down to check his footing. Don't jerk him in the mouth by mistake.

Trail riding often involves going up and down hills. This can be hard on your horse, especially if you're bumping around on his back like a sack of potatoes. Sitting in the correct position can make his job easier. When going up a hill, lean your upper body forward a bit and lift your rear end slightly out of the saddle. Hold your reins about halfway up your horse's neck and keep them loose. Your horse needs to be able to stretch without your pulling on his mouth. Leaning slightly forward takes your weight off his hindquarters so he can use them to push himself up the hill. Don't crouch too far forward over your horse's neck, however, because this can unbalance him and make it awkward to step up. Often horses like to race uphill, but it's important that you make your horse walk or jog slowly and carefully. It doesn't do your horse's legs any good to go tearing off at top speed up a hill because it can cause sprains and strains. If the hill is really steep, give your horse a break halfway. Let him stand sideways, as level as possible, for a few minutes to catch his breath.

When riding downhill, stand in the stirrups so you are light in the saddle. Push your heels down and put most of your weight in the stirrups. Push your feet more forward than usual. Keep your legs close to your horse's sides and lean back slightly—not so much that you plop your rear in the saddle. This puts too much weight on his hindquarters and may make him slip and slide down the hill. Keep a soft but firm contact on your horse's mouth so he doesn't speed up or lose his balance down the hill.

Safety on the Trail

Here are some easy-to-remember tips to keep you and your horse safe on the trail:

- Tell someone at the barn where you're going. If your horse comes back by himself, the search party will know where to look.
- Carry a cellular phone or change for a phone call.
- Carry a hoof pick in a pocket or tie it to a ring on your saddle. Rocks or mud in your horse's hooves could make him lame.
- If you want to stop on the trail to picnic or rest, carry a lead rope on your saddle and put a halter under your horse's bridle. Then you can take the bridle off and safely tie your horse to rest or munch on grass. Never tie him with the reins unless it is an emergency because he could pull back and break them.

- Carry your driver's license or some other form of identification in a pocket.
- If it's hot, carry a plastic bottle full of water so you can drink if you feel dehydrated.
- Have a dog tag engraved with your name and phone number and attach it to a ring on your saddle.
- Respect other people's property. Don't ride over crops or plants or near cattle or other livestock.
- Always shut gates behind you.
- Always make your horse walk the last half mile back to the barn after a trail ride. If you always return at top speed, your horse will jig about when you try to make him walk.

Riding on the Road

In an ideal world, you wouldn't have to ride on or near roads, but many horses are kept in the suburbs or in residential areas, and you might have to travel on a road to get to a trail. If that's the case, it's best to walk on the far right with traffic, and if there is a grassy shoulder on the road, stay on it. If you're out in a group, ride in single file.

Unfortunately, very few drivers understand horses or realize they are easily spooked. They may even yell, wave, or honk their horns at you. Many cars pass you with only inches to spare, so be prepared and ride defensively. A few drivers may slow down, but don't count on it. If someone is really speeding toward you, hold up your hand and ask the driver to slow down.

Passing Scary Objects

Stay alert when trail riding and take note of things that might scare your horse so you'll be prepared if he spooks. If a horse has too much energy, he may spook at a lot of things. Something as harmless as a piece of paper blowing around may frighten him.

A halter under your horse's bridle is a good safety measure on the trail.

Cattle, tractors, pigs, clotheslines, sheep, birds, and donkeys can all reduce some horses to shivering, snorting wrecks or cause them to bolt.

If you spot something that could make your horse spook, it is imperative that you stay completely calm and don't transmit any nervousness to him. If he senses that you're scared about something, he may get worked up too. Keep a firm hold on the reins, squeeze with both legs, and ask him to walk forward. Don't allow him to run away from the object or veer off the trail. Reward your horse for taking a step toward the scary object with your voice and a pat. Be patient and allow your horse time to get over his fear. And never, ever get off your horse if you have to walk by a frightening object. It's safer to stay in the saddle; otherwise, if your horse spooks or bolts, you could get trampled or knocked over.

Riding in a Group

One of the best things about owning a horse is being able to ride in the company of friends. However, before you head out, remember that it can be very exciting for a horse to be with other horses outside of the ring, and he may behave differently from how he does normally. Even the quietest horse may suddenly experience an extra burst of energy the second he steps into a field or onto a trail. Be prepared for frisky or naughty behavior.

You may need to use stronger equipment than you use in the arena, especially if you're going to lope or gallop in company. For example, you may want to use a curb bit instead of a snaffle or use a tie-down so he can't throw his head in the air to avoid contact with the bit.

When riding with others, keep your distance, if possible. If you're riding single file, keep one horse length between you. You don't want to get kicked. If you're riding next to someone, stay about 3 feet apart. Don't lag behind the group because your horse may run to catch up. Try to maintain your position in the group.

Don't allow your horse to run away from scary objects.

Be respectful of other riders when going out in a group.

Don't zoom past others because you could upset their horses. If you want to pass another horse, ask permission or call out "passing." If you see something potentially dangerous such as wire or glass on the ground, warn your trail mates.

When heading out on the trail, stick to a slow pace at first. See how the horses get along. If one is frisky or misbehaving, the rest of the horses may act up too. Decide as a group if you want to jog, lope, or gallop. Don't take off without warning. Give all the riders time to get secure in the saddle and shorten their reins for more control. Once you set off at a faster pace, pay attention to the rest of the group. If someone is having problems controlling his horse, the whole group should slow down until that person is in control again. If one horse bolts, it's likely the others will get excited and bolt too. This can be really dangerous on a trail, especially if the footing is bad or the ground is uneven.

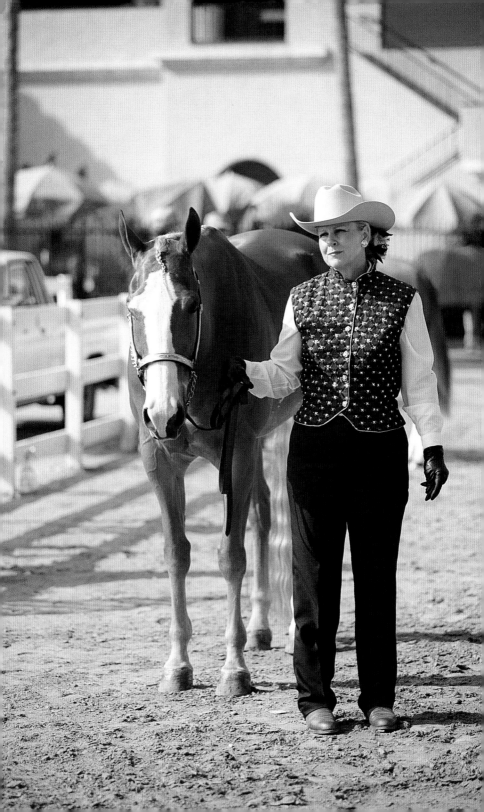

8

Showing Your Horse

Taking your horse to a show is one way to see how productive your workouts at home have been. A competition is a great place to show off all you've taught your horse, and it's a super opportunity to test your own riding skills. It's also your chance to wear the latest show apparel. One of the best things about showing is that you may even come home with a ribbon or two. But showing can be a challenge. You may practice something over and over at home until your horse does it perfectly, but when you do the same thing at a show, things might not go as planned. Performing in front of a crowd and an eagle-eyed judge can be a nerve-racking experience. Nearly all competitors get "show nerves," and if you're new to showing, you may feel anxious, which may make your horse tense. She may not obey your cues, and she might act up during a class. It's best not to worry too much about your horse's behavior at this stage. The more shows you attend together, the more experienced you'll become, and soon showing will be a fun, satisfying experience.

Horse shows take place year-round. To find out about shows in your area, look for "premiums" (the show schedule of classes) at your local tack shop. Check local free horse magazines for show information too. If you board your horse at a big facility, there may be shows on-site so you won't have to travel. If you want to go to a show at another barn but don't have a trailer, perhaps you could hire a professional hauler with several barn mates. Your trainer may be able to arrange your horse's transport to a show, too. Trainers often take groups of students to shows.

Showing lets you know how productive your workouts at home have been.

There are many different types of show classes, and at least one should suit you and your horse. If your horse is slow, steady, and well behaved, she may do well in western pleasure classes. If she's quick and athletic, she may excel at speed events such as barrel racing. If she has been trained to work livestock, you could give cutting or team penning a go. And if your horse is a fine example of a particular breed, you can show her off in breed-only classes or shows. If you ride with a trainer, ask her what classes she thinks you and your horse should try.

It is essential that your horse be well mannered at home before you take her to a show. If she misbehaves in the ring, the judge will

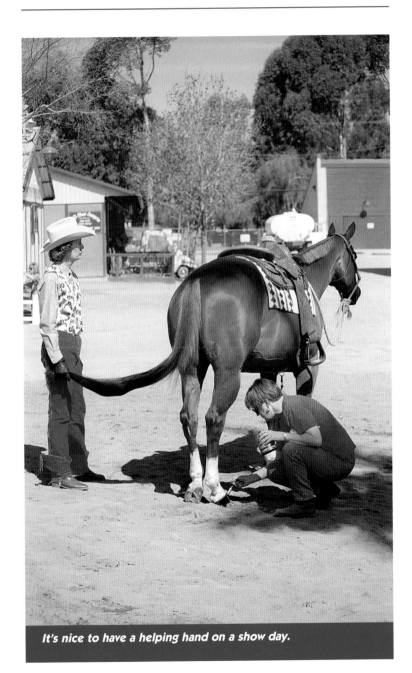

It's nice to have a helping hand on a show day.

mark you down, and you are bound to feel embarrassed. If you're not sure how your horse will react at a show, take her to a few shows, but don't enter any classes. Simply walk around and let her get used to the hustle and bustle of the show ground. Let her eat a meal there, or munch on grass. You can also lunge her or walk her around the warm-up arena a couple of times.

Preparing Your Horse

Judges expect to see your horse well turned out at a show, but getting her to look immaculate can take weeks of preparation. You don't just pull your horse out of the field and expect to win. Success takes some elbow grease. If you go to a show, notice how all the horses shine. This comes from three things: a good diet, a lot of grooming, and coat conditioners. If your horse is fed correctly, her coat should have a natural shine. If it doesn't, add a vitamin supplement and about half a cup of corn oil to her daily diet. You will also need to brush her every day to remove old hair and stimulate the natural oils in her skin. On the day of the show, give her coat extra sparkle by spraying her with a sheen product. Oil her hooves before you enter a class, too.

Most western show horses have fairly short manes. If your horse's mane is long and unruly, shorten it with special trimming scissors and then pull it with a mane comb so it looks neat, yet natural. The mane should be about 3 inches long and fall on the right side. Most savvy competitors "band" their horse's mane for a show, which makes the mane look neater, and accentuates the horse's topline. They separate the mane into many narrow sections and fasten each one with a band. Shave a bridle path at the top of the mane, too. It should be 3 to 6 inches. Most riders leave the tail long and flowing but it should always be spotlessly clean and free of tangles.

Trim your horse's legs and fetlocks so they look streamlined, and use electric clippers to remove whiskers around her muzzle and the shaggy hair under her chin. Western show horses typically have all fur clipped out of their ears. If you remove this hair, be sure to give your horse protection from flies and gnats with a fly bonnet and fly spray.

What Your Horse Should Wear

Some competitors own show saddles that are adorned with a lot of silver trim, but new riders can use their everyday tack as long as it's clean and in good shape. Your horse should sport a western saddle, cinch, and saddle pad. Her bridle can be the one-ear, two-ear, or browband style, and it should be made of leather. Bosals, breastplates, and tie-downs can be used in most classes. If you're unsure about what your horse can or cannot wear in a class, question the show manager or write to USA Equestrian, the governing body for equine competition.

What You Should Wear

The clothes you wear during a show depend on the class you're entering. While the requirements are fairly basic in premise, some classes can turn out to be quite a fashion show. For pleasure and horsemanship classes, men usually wear a neat, western-style, button-down shirt. Some competitors wear a scarf tied with a square knot, too. Today's current trends for women are "slinky tops": form fitting long sleeved knitwear. These are worn alone, or with jackets or vests. Most women wear show pants—a form-fitting type of dress slacks—under chaps, although jeans are the norm for men (and are permissible for women). Fringed leather chaps top off the outfit of most rail classes.

If you're competing your horse in-hand, such as in halter or showmanship classes, women generally wear a smart blazer and show pants, as chaps aren't worn in an unmounted class. A west-

Your show clothes can reflect your personal style.

ern hat—made of fur felt or tightly woven straw—and roper style boots are a must, and women should pull their hair back into a tidy ponytail or bun.

What you wear to compete depends largely on your own personal style and taste. Consider your horse's coloring when you outfit yourself. Go to a couple of shows and see how the competitors dress. Stick to simple, flattering clothes that complement your horse's coat. For example, horses with warm tones in their coats (chestnuts, sorrels, duns) look great in neutrals and browns. Bays, blacks, grays and blue roans can wear jewel tones nicely. When in doubt, black is always a safe bet. But remember, you don't want

A western pleasure horse must be well balanced at all speeds.

your outfit to be better than your riding skills, so have the judge remember your horsemanship, not your clothes.

Western Show Classes

Now that you and your horse are ready to show, here are some points to remember. When competing in a rail class, it's important to show off your horse to the judge. The judge usually stands in the middle of the ring, and you stay as close to the rail as possible. Maintain your eye on the judge and the horses around you. Keep some distance between you and the horse in front. If you get too close to someone, pass the individual on the inside or circle in a corner to create space. However, do this sparingly. When you ride in front of the judge, your position should be picture perfect and your horse should be moving forward at a nice, steady pace. Never pass anybody who is in front of the judge. This is considered extremely rude.

Now you're ready to check out some popular show classes to see which ones suit you and your horse best.

Western Pleasure

Western Pleasure is a class that can be enjoyed by riders of every level. Basically, your horse is judged on the way she moves and behaves. She must obey your cues instantly and appear well balanced at all speeds. Her gaits need to be flowing, rhythmic, and consistent. She should also be calm, quiet, obedient, and should look as if she is a pleasant horse to be around. The judge will ask you to walk, jog, and lope in both directions around the ring, and you must ride your horse on a fairly loose rein to demonstrate how well behaved and responsive she is.

Western Horsemanship, or Equitation

In this class your riding skills are judged. It usually consists of two parts: riding on the rail with the rest of the competitors and

Trail classes test your horse's obedience.

performing an individual test. You must demonstrate control over your horse and skill in performing specific movements. First you are asked to walk, jog, and lope in a group, then you line up and wait to perform your individual test. The test is usually posted outside the arena before the class. You may be asked to do several transitions, some figure eights, and to ride down the center line.

Trail

Trail classes test your horse's obedience and skill on the trail. A course is set up in the ring, and your horse must travel through it calmly and sensibly on a loose rein. You have to step over poles at the walk and jump small fences at the jog or lope. You also have to back up and halt inside a line of poles and walk over a small wooden bridge. You might have to open and shut a gate in a more advanced trail class. You are judged on your horse's performance over the obstacles, her manners, her attitude, and her response to your cues.

Reining

In reining classes, you perform a set pattern in the arena before a judge. The National Reining Horse Association's patterns include loping and galloping in circles, flying lead changes, 360-degree spins, sliding stops from the gallop, and rollbacks, which are when a horse stops and makes a 180-degree turn at the lope or gallop. These are advanced movements that take time to learn and practice. You have to ride your horse with a loose rein, and she must listen to the subtle cues you give her with your weight, seat, and legs and respond immediately. She has to be nimble, quick, and able to slow down, speed up, or stop instantly.

Barrel Racing

Barrel racing is a timed speed event in which you must gallop around three barrels in a cloverleaf pattern. The barrels are usually 120 feet apart. Your horse has to stop, start, and gallop

You may have to gallop during your test in a reining class.

quickly, and she must be brave, athletic, and agile. She also has to know how to do flying lead changes because she'll need to switch leads at top speed. You enter the arena at a flat-out gallop, then slow down to circle the first barrel, staying as close to it as possible to save time. Next you pick up speed to reach the second barrel, and slow down again to go around it. This routine is repeated for the third barrel, and when your horse has finished circling, she must gallop at a breakneck pace over the finish line. You should put splint boots and bell boots on your horse's legs to protect her in case she kicks herself or overreaches and hits her front pasterns with her back hooves while gallop-

Barrel racing horses must be nimble and speedy.

ing. Also, you have to ride in a forward seat with your rear end slightly out of the saddle so your horse can use her hindquarters to propel herself forward.

Working Cow Horse

In the working cow horse class, you work a single cow or steer with your horse. This means you and your horse must control the movement of the cow in the arena. When you enter the arena, you perform a quick reining pattern for the judge. Then a cow is released into the arena. You then demonstrate tasks including "boxing the cow"—making her stay at one end of the arena, galloping her both ways around the arena near the fence, and making her go around in a circle in both directions. At most events, this must be done in two minutes.

To be a successful working cow horse, your horse has to listen to your cues and watch what the cow is doing too. She has to be able to control the cow without upsetting her. Experienced horses crouch down and watch the cow with an eagle eye, and they appear to follow its movements without any cues from their riders. A working cow horse is judged on several things, including her ability to stay well balanced, change direction smoothly, and effectively work the cow.

Cutting

In a cutting class, you are faced with a herd of about two dozen cows. You must drive several cows out of the herd, select one, bring her out in the open arena, and work her by herself. This all takes place in two and a half minutes. You're allowed to have helpers in the arena—usually two "herd holders" who keep the herd at the back of the arena and two "turn-back" riders who encourage the cow to face you and your horse.

Your horse is supposed to work the cow by herself, using skill and natural instinct (sometimes called "cow sense"). The judge wants to see your horse crouch down and match the cow step for step, so you'll lose points if you have to cue your horse with the reins. The goal is to finish in the middle of the arena with your horse facing the cow. It is truly amazing to watch an experienced cutting horse in action. Such a horse appears to read the cow's mind.

Team Penning

If you have two friends who like working cattle as much as you do, get together and try team penning. A team of three horses and riders gallop toward a small group of cows, sort three desig-

In a cutting horse class, your horse must be able to shadow a cow's every movement.

nated cows from the herd, and round them in a paddock at the opposite end of the arena. Generally, a rider enters the herd by herself and cuts one calf at a time. Her teammates turn back strays and help keep the selected calf moving toward the pen. This timed event is officiated by two judges who mark each team for accuracy and efficiency.

Halter

In the halter class you bring your horse into the ring with a lead rope, chain, and halter, and you line up in front of the judge. The judge studies your horse's overall look, muscles, fitness, and conformation. Then the judge asks you to jog your horse in front of her so she can watch the horse's movement. A halter class is a bit like a beauty contest for horses. During the class, you must ask your horse to stand square, and try to keep her head up and her ears forward. You should have to "arrange" her only once. Judges don't like it when you fuss with your horse's legs or head during the class. To be a winner in halter classes, both you and your horse should give off a proud, positive image in the ring.

Saddle Up and Go!

By now you should have a basic understanding of the skills you need to learn in order to be an effective western rider. You should be able to mount a horse and know the subtle cues that ask her to walk, jog, and lope. And if you've been working hard in the saddle, the horse actually does everything you ask her to do! It's a great feeling when you realize that all of the lessons you have taken and all of the time you have spent riding have really paid off.

You've become a competent rider. Now the fun really begins. You can head out on long trail rides with friends, knowing full well that you can handle any situation that may arise. You can enter the show ring and feel confident that you and your horse will give a good performance. And most importantly, you'll be able to mount a horse you've never ridden before, knowing deep down that no matter what she does or how she acts, you are capable enough to ride her.

What are you waiting for? Zip up those chaps, find yourself a horse, and start riding!

Resources

American Association of Equine
Practitioners
4075 Iron Works Parkway
Lexington, KY 40511
(859) 233-0147
www.aaep.org

American Connemara Pony
Society
2360 Hunting Ridge Road
Winchester, VA 22603
(540) 662-5953
www.acps.org

American Driving Society
2324 Clark Road
Lapeer, MI 48446
(810) 664-8666
www.americandrivingsociety.org

American Endurance Ride
Conference
P.O. 6027
Auburn, CA 95604
(866) 271-AERC
www.aerc.org

American Farriers Association
4059 Iron Works Parkway
Suite 1
Lexington, KY 40511
(859) 233-7411
www.amfarriers.com

American Hanoverian
Society
4067 Iron Works Parkway

Suite 1
Lexington, KY 40511
(859) 255-4141
www.hanoverian.org

American Holsteiner Horse
Association
222 E. Main Street #1
Georgetown, KY 40324-1712
(502) 863-4239
www.holsteiner.com

American Horse Council
1616 H Street NW
7th Floor
Washington, D.C. 20006
(202) 296-4031
www.horsecouncil.org

American Horse Protection
Association
1000 29th Street
#T-100
Washington, D.C. 20007-3820
(202) 965-0500

USA Equestrian (formerly
American Horse Shows
Association)
4047 Iron Works Parkway
Lexington, KY 40511-8483
(859) 258-2472
www.equestrian.org

American Morgan Horse
Association
P.O. Box 960

Shelburne, VT 05482
802-985-4944
www.morganhorse.com

American Mustang and Burro
Association
P.O. Box 788
Lincoln, CA 95648
(530) 633-9271
www.bardalisa.com

American Paint Horse
Association
P.O. Box 961023
Fort Worth, TX 76161-0023
(817) 834-APHA
www.apha.com

American Quarter Horse
Association
P.O. Box 200
Amarillo, TX 79168
(806) 376-4811
www.aqha.com

American Riding Instructors
Association
28801 Trenton Court
Bonita Springs, FL 34134-3337
(239) 948-3232
www.riding-instructor.com

American Saddlebred Horse
Association
4093 Iron Works Parkway
Lexington, KY 40511
(859) 259-2742
www.asha.net

American Trails
P.O. Box 491797
Redding, CA 96049-1797
(530) 547-2060
www.americantrails.org

American Trakehner Association
1514 West Church Street
Newark, OH 43055
(740) 344-1111
www.americantrakehner.com

American Warmblood
Society
2 Buffalo Run Road
Center Ridge, AR 72027
(501) 893-2777
www.americanwarmblood.org

American Youth Horse
Council
577 N. Boyero Avenue
Pueblo West, CO 81007
(800) TRY-AYHC
www.ayhc.com

Appaloosa Horse Club, Inc.
2720 West Pullman Road
Moscow, ID 83843
(208) 882-5578
www.appaloosa.com

Arabian Horse Registry of
America
10805 East Bethany Drive
Aurora, CO 80014
(303) 696-4500
www.theregistry.org

The Bureau of Livestock
Identification
1220 N Street
Room A-130
Sacramento, CA 95814
(916) 654-0889
www.cdfa.ca.gov/ahfss.li/

CHA - The Association for
Horsemanship Safety and
Education
5318 Old Bullard Road
Tyler, TX 75703
(800) 399-0138
www.cha-ahse.org

Intercollegiate Horse Show
Association
P.O. Box 741
Stonybrook, NY 11790-0741
(303) 450-4774
www.ihsa.com

The Jockey Club
821 Corporate Drive
Lexington, KY 40503-2794
(859) 224-2700
www.jockeyclub.com

National Cutting Horse
Association
260 Bailey Avenue
Fort Worth, TX 76107-1862
(817) 244-6188
www.nchacutting.com

National 4-H Council
7100 Connecticut Avenue
Chevy Chase, MD 20815

(301) 961-2959
www.fourhcouncil.edu

National Hunter and Jumper
Association
P.O. Box 1015
Riverside, CT 06878
(203) 869-1225
www.nhja.com

National Reining Horse
Association
3000 NW 10th Street
Oklahoma City, OK 73107-5302
(405) 946-7400
www.nrha.com

North American Riding for the
Handicapped Association
P.O. Box 33150
Denver, CO 80233
(303) 452-1212
www.narha.org

Palomino Horse Breeders of
America
15253 East Skelly Drive
Tulsa, OK 74116-2637
www.palominohba.com

Performance Horse Registry
4047 Iron Works Parkway
Lexington, KY 40511
(859) 231-6662
www.phr.com

Swedish Warmblood Association
of North America
P.O. Box 788

Socorro, NM 87801
(505) 835-1318
www.wbstallions.com/wb/swana

Tennessee Walking Horse
Breeders' and Exhibitors'
Association
P.O. Box 286
Lewisburg, TN 37091-0286
(931) 359-1574
www.twhbea.com

Trail Riders of Today
P.O. Box 30033
Bethesda, MD 20824-0033
(301) 854-3467
www.trot-md.org

United States Combined Training
Association
525 Old Waterford Road NW
Leesburg, VA 20176
(703) 779-0440
www.eventingusa.com

United States Dressage
Federation
220 Lexington Green Circle
Lexington, KY 40503
(859) 971-2277
www.usdf.org

United State Equestrian
Team
P.O. Box 355
Gladstone, NJ 07934
(908) 234-1251
www.uset.com

United States Pony Club
4041 Iron Works Parkway
Lexington, KY 40511-8462
(859) 254-7669
www.ponyclub.org

United States Team Penning
Association
P.O. Box 4170
Fort Worth, TX 76164-0170
(817) 378-8082
www.ustpa.com

Western Stock Show Association
4655 Humboldt Street
Denver, CO 80216
(303) 297-1166

Glossary

aids: The communication signals given from a rider to a horse.

barrel: The area of a horse's body between the fore- and hindquarters.

barrel racing: A timed contest in which a mounted rider makes sharp turns around three barrels set in a cloverleaf pattern.

bosal: A type of hackamore bridle with a simple noseband made of leather or rope attached to a large knot under the horse's chin.

breastplate: Also known as a breastband or breast collar; a device used across a horse's chest that attaches to the saddle and prevents it from slipping.

bridle: A head harness used to control and guide a horse when driving or riding; usually consists of a headstall and reins with a bit.

canter: A three-beat gait that resembles a slow gallop.

chaps: Leggings worn over trousers (in western riding attire) offering protection against brush, thorns, and cold or wet weather.

cinch: The western term for girth, which is a band that encircles a horse's belly to hold a saddle on the horse's back.

crop: A short riding whip with a looped lash.

curb bit: A bit with various mouthpieces and shanks, usually with a center rise that shifts pressure from the tongue to the roof of the mouth.

cutting: A western event during which a horse and rider have 2 minutes to separate an individual calf or cow from the rest of its herd and keep it in the middle of the pen.

deaden: To desensitize a horse's mouth or sides by excessive use of the aids.

diagonal: The movement of a forefoot in unison with the opposite hind foot.

diagonal pair: A pair of a horse's legs consisting of a foreleg and the hind leg of the opposite side.

fetlock: A joint that makes a projection on the back of a horse's lower leg above the back of the hoof.

green horse: A horse, usually a young one, who is inexperienced and not fully trained.

gymkhana games: Informal games, contests, and races on horseback.

hackamore: A type of bridle with a noseband that applies pressure on the nose for control instead of using a standard mouthpiece for control.

headstall: The pieces of a bridle including the cheekstrap, throatclatch, browband, and noseband if used.

high-stepping it: Slang for lifting the legs with great animation.

horn: The projection above the raised part in front of a western saddle.

jog: A horse's slow, measured trot.

lasso: A 30- to 40-foot-long rope with a running noose used for catching horses and cattle.

leading rein: Lifting one rein in an outward direction to encourage the horse to turn his or her head.

lead: The action by the forefoot that takes the first step when entering a canter and while cantering and galloping; a horse on the correct lead is on the right lead when circling the clockwise and on the left lead when circling counter-clockwise.

loose rein: A rein that hangs loosely without any pulling or contact between the rider's hands and the horse's mouth.

lope: A natural, easy horse gait that is faster than a jog; it has a four-beat rhythm with a pause after the fourth beat.

lunge: To train or exercise your horse with a lunge line, a whip, and your voice.

lunge line: A rein made of cotton or nylon, about 25 feet long, that attaches to a horse's halter.

neck reining: A way of guiding a horse with reins. A mounted rider holds both reins in one hand (usually to the left) and steers the horse by pulling the reins in the direction he or she wants to turn.

position: The carriage of a rider's body in the saddle.

post: To rise and sit in rhythm with the horse's trot while riding.

rein hand: The hand that is holding both reins, usually the left hand in western-style riding.

romal: A whip that is attached to a pair of closed reins.

roping: The act of lassoing cattle.

snaffle bit: A type of mild bit.

split reins: Western-style reins that do not join at their ends.

spur: A pointed device that attaches to a rider's heel and is used as an aid to urge a horse to move by gently pressing the spur into the horse's side.

tack (tackle): Saddle, bridle, and other equipment used in riding and handling a horse.

team penning: A timed sport in which a team of three riders tries to cut three numbered calves out of a herd of thirty and pen them at a designated end of an arena.

transition: A change of pace from one type of movement to another.

tree (saddletree): The frame of a saddle.

withers: The highest part of a horse's back, where the neck and the back join.

Author Lesley Ward has combined her talent in writing for the beginner with the wisdom of *Horse Illustrated* to bring this definitive guide to all beginning riders. *The* Horse Illustrated *Guide to Western Riding* covers the fundamentals—from loping and galloping to trail riding and showing. Complete with step-by-step instructions, countless tips, full-color photos, and an easy-to-use glossary, this book takes the guesswork out of western riding.

The *Horse Illustrated* **Guide** series is designed to help the novice establish and maintain one of the most rewarding relationships—that between person and horse.

Collect the Whole Series!
More horse facts at www.horseillustrated.com

About the Author

Lesley Ward is the editor of *Young Rider*, a magazine dedicated to teaching young people, in an easy-to-read and entertaining way, how to properly look after their horses and safely improve their riding skills.

She is also the author of: *Your Healthy & Happy Horse: How to Care for Your Horse and Have Fun Too*, *Let's Go to a Show: How to Win Ribbons and Have Fun Too*, and many others.

Lesley enjoys eventing and trail-riding her horse, Murphy, and teaching children how to ride on her farm in Lexington, Kentucky.

BOWTIE
P R E S S®
A Division of BowTie, Inc.
Irvine, California

ISBN 1-931993-17-3